Substitute Teaching: Planning for Success

Elizabeth S. Manera
General Editor

Kappa Delta Pi, an International Honor Society in Education

West Lafayette, Indiana

Founded 1911

Publisher	Kappa Delta Pi, an International Honor Society in Education
Executive Director	Michael P. Wolfe
Acting Director of Publications	Grant E. Mabie
Copy Editor	Carol Bloom
Editors	Marji E. Gold-Vukson
	Jennifer L. Kapp
	Grant E. Mabie
	Leslie S. Rebhorn
Editorial Assistants	Patti L. Cox
	Marji E. Gold-Vukson
	Jamie Danesi
	Linda A. Heaton
	Nadia Ibrahim
	Victoria Cox Kaser
Designers	Angela Bruntlett
	Denise Miller Trulley
Cartoonist	Dave Sattler of Lafayette, Indiana

ii

Library of Congress Cataloging-in-Publication Data

Manera, Elizabeth S., ed.
    Substitute teaching: Planning for success/Elizabeth S. Manera, general editor.
    p. cm. Includes bibliographical references.
    ISBN 0-912099-06-2 (pbk.) $20.00
    1. Substitute teachers—United States
    2. Teaching—Vocational guidance—United States. I. Manera, Elizabeth S.
           LB2844.1.S8S827 1996
           371.1'4122—dc20
           96-26437
           CIP

Printed in the United States of America.

01 00   5 4 3

Kappa Delta Pi, an International Honor Society in Education, is dedicated to scholarship and excellence in education. The Society, as a community of scholars pledged to worthy ideals:

- Recognizes scholarship and excellence in education;

- Promotes the development and dissemination of worthy educational ideas and practices;

- Enhances the continuous growth and leadership of its diverse membership; and

- Maintains a high degree of professional fellowship.

Kappa Delta Pi invites to membership such persons who exhibit commendable personal qualities, worthy educational ideals, and sound scholarship, without regard to race, color, religion, or sex. The Society's members represent "the best and brightest" in education: from every adult age group, from educators at prekindergarten to college and university levels, and now in more than 90 countries; from education major to classroom teacher to principal to professor of education— comprising a truly intergenerational and international educational honor society.

iii

Chapter Authors

1 & 2   **Elizabeth S. Manera**
Emeritus Professor of Secondary Education
Arizona State University
Tempe, Arizona

Mary L. Harthun
Department Chair for Staff Development
Phoenix Union High School District
Phoenix, Arizona

Terri St. Michel
High School English Teacher
South Mountain High School
Phoenix Union High School District
Phoenix, Arizona

3 & 4   Elizabeth S. Manera

Donovan Cook
Coordinator of Student Field Experiences
Assistant Professor of Education
Washburn University
Topeka, Kansas

Kay W. Terry
Assistant Professor of Education
Western Kentucky University
Bowling Green, Kentucky

5   Polly Wolfe
Former Classroom Teacher
Assistant Professor of Art Education
Ball State University
Muncie, Indiana

6   Patricia Phelps
Associate Professor
University of Central Arkansas
Conway, Arkansas

7   Patricia Phelps

8   Elizabeth S. Manera

Kay Hartwell-Hunicutt
Associate Professor of Education and Law
Arizona State University
Tempe, Arizona

Lesson Plan Contributors

1 Choosing the Main Idea
Gloria J. Shelton
25 years in teaching
Grade 2 Teacher
Taft Elementary School
Lawton Public Schools
Lawton, Oklahoma

2 Pick, Choose, and Group Categorization
Debra I. Gowins
5 years in teaching
Kindergarten Teacher
Natcher Elementary School
Warren County Schools
Bowling Green, Kentucky

3 Writing about Dinosaurs
Amy Somerville
Former Substitute Teacher
Grade 1 Teacher
Bransford Elementary School
Robertson County Schools
Springfield, Tennessee

4 Counting Coins
Merri Lynne Hinton
Library Media Specialist
South Todd Elementary School
Todd County Schools
Guthrie, Kentucky

5 Building a Better Airplane
Steven W. Sanders
3 years in teaching
Grades 4–5 Science Teacher
L. C. Curry Elementary School
Bowling Green Independent Schools
Bowling Green, Kentucky

6 Learning Lines of Latitude
Richard A. Rutherford
3 years in teaching
Grade 5 Teacher
Francis Vigo Elementary School
Vincennes, Indiana

7 Playing Beach Ball Volleyball
Kathy Bristow
24 years in teaching
Middle School Physical Education Teacher
Edgewood Middle School
North Shore District #112
Highland Park, Illinois

8 Identifying Shapes Musically
Peggy Tordoff
24 years in teaching
Former Substitute Teacher
1975 Louisiana Teacher of the Year
Kindergarten Teacher
Ball Elementary School
Rapides Parish School System
Pineville, Louisiana

9 Manipulating Space
Micheal Gold-Vukson
15 years in teaching
Elementary Art Teacher
Edgelea, Miller, Murdock, and Washington Elementary Schools
Lafayette School Corporation
Lafayette, Indiana

10 Predicting What's in the Box
Donna M. Viveiros
25 years in teaching
1986 Massachusetts Teacher of the Year
Grade 6 Teacher
Fall River Public Schools
Fall River, Massachusetts

11 Identifying Kinds of Writing
Griselle M. Diaz-Gemmati
15 years in teaching
Former Substitute Teacher
Grades 7–8 Language Arts, Social Studies, and Math Teacher
1993 Golden Apple Fellow
Norwood Park School
Chicago Public Schools
Chicago, Illinois

12 Creating a Planet
Lynda Hatch
16 years in K–12 teaching
1982 Oregon Teacher of the Year
6 years in college teaching
Assistant Professor of Education
Northern Arizona University
Flagstaff, Arizona

13 Interpreting Tables
Patricia Powell
3 years in teaching
Grade 6 Teacher
East Ridge Middle School
Hamilton County School System
Chattanooga, Tennessee

14 Conducting an Experiment
Dixie Carpenter
20 years in teaching
Grade 7 Science Teacher
Challenger Middle School
Glendale Elementary School District #40
Glendale, Arizona

15 Understanding Population Density
Connie J. Dwyer
14 years in teaching
Grade 7 Teacher
London Middle School
London City Schools
London, Ohio

16 Analyzing Advertising
Janet L. Henke
23 years in teaching
Grade 6–8 Mentor Teacher
Old Court Middle School
Baltimore County Schools
Baltimore, Maryland

Russell G. Henke
24 years in education
Former Classroom Teacher
Coordinator of Health Education
Montgomery County Public Schools
Rockville, Maryland

17 Playing Matball
Pam Eckhardt
26 years in teaching
Grades 6–8 Physical Education Teacher
Eagleview Middle School
Academy School District #20
Colorado Springs, Colorado

18 Solving Problems Creatively
Polly Wolfe

19 Building Strong Communication Skills
Nancy Day
21 years in teaching
Former Home Economics Teacher
K–6 Guidance Counselor
Enon Elementary School
Hustead Elementary School
Mad River-Green Local Schools
Springfield, Ohio

20 Conducting a Survey
Helen Follis
19 years in teaching
Grade 5 Teacher
Buck Lake Elementary School
Leon County Schools
Tallahassee, Florida

21 Writing Clear Directions
Terrie St. Michel

22 Creating a Character
Lori D'Achino Bucco
13 years in teaching
Grade 11 English Teacher
Falls Church High School
Fairfax County Public Schools
Falls Church, Virginia

23 Correcting Algebra Mistakes
Hazel H. Orth
22 years in teaching
High School Mathematics Teacher
Langley High School
Fairfax County Schools
McLean, Virginia

24 Building Molecules
Joan E. Vallee
25 years in teaching
Former Physics and Chemistry Teacher
1985 Louisiana Teacher of the Year
Assistant Professor of Chemistry
McNeese State University
Lake Charles, Louisiana

25 Reporting the News
Kathleen Estep
26 years in teaching
High School Social Studies Teacher
Greenon High School
Mad River-Green Local Schools
Springfield, Ohio

26 Practicing the Language
Mary L. Harthun

27 Improving Fitness with Ultimate Frisbee
M. Linda Nickson
18 years in teaching
High School Physical Education Teacher
Stow High School
Stow City Schools
Stow, Ohio

28 Analyzing Rehearsals
Dan Bruce
9 years in teaching
Choral Director
Pullman High School
Pullman School District #267
Pullman, Washington

29 Constructing a House
Betsey Moore
7 years in substitute teaching
24 additional years in education
Performance Consultant
Memorial Health Alliance
Mount Holly, New Jersey

30 Mapping Concepts
Jan Fall
24 years in education
K–12 Gifted and Talented Coordinator
Rochester Public Schools
Rochester, Minnesota

Jan Smith
26 years in teaching
High School English and Reading Teacher
Mayo High School
Rochester Public Schools
Rochester, Minnesota

Lesson Modifications for Students with Special Needs
Debra Kay Lynch
Former Elementary Special Education Teacher
Assistant Professor of Special Education
Kutztown University
Kutztown, Pennsylvania

v

Reviewers

Barbara S. Arnold
Reading Communications Teacher
Indian Valley Middle School
Enon, Ohio

John E. Bell
Professor Emeritus
Arizona State University
Tempe, Arizona

Bernice G. Brown
Professor of Education
Slippery Rock University
Slippery Rock, Pennsylvania

Lisa Cummaro
Elementary School Teacher
St. Gregory's Catholic School
Plantation, Florida

Vicki A. Green
Professor of Social and Curriculum
Studies
Okanagan University College
Kelowna, British Columbia, Canada

Susan Wolfe Hecht
History Teacher
Hamilton High School
Los Angeles, California

Wendy Markus
Substitute Teacher
Kalamazoo, Michigan

Jeannie N. Parscal
Instructor and Coordinator
Butler County Community College
El Dorado, Kansas

Kimberly S. Roberts
Grade 6 Teacher
Mormon Trail Community Shool
Garden Grove, Iowa

Mary Lou Sullenger
Substitute Elementary Teacher
Plainfield, Indiana

Rachel Z. Thomae
Substitute Teacher
Garden School District
Sandy, Utah

Carolyn R. Wactler
Faculty Associate and College
Supervisor
Arizona State University
Tempe, Arizona

Special Thanks

As greater demands are placed upon teachers with higher expectations for students' learning, the job of a substitute teacher has become more important. Valuable classroom time cannot be wasted with a substitute merely "baby-sitting." Acknowledging this situation, the substitute teacher has one of the most difficult assignments in the schools. Therefore, the Association of Teacher Educators in 1992, under the guidance of Shirley Robards, established a Commission to review the status of substitute teaching in the United States and make recommendations to the Association for future action.

A number of projects were developed during the Commission's three-year tenure. A national survey was conducted to identify the status of substitute teaching. Sample activities were developed for college and university educators to use in their preservice teacher education classes or with student teachers. In addition, college courses, workshops, and substitute teacher handbooks for individual school districts were also developed.

This book also evolved as one of those projects. Therefore, it is with deep appreciation that the editor and authors of *Substitute Teaching: Planning for Success* acknowledge the research and labor that members of the ATE Commission completed that allowed this handbook to evolve from its original form. The members of the ATE Substitute Teacher Commission who contributed to the initial development of this work include:

Renee Barstack	Christy Hooser	Kathy Bristow	Lyle Mottinger
David Bell	James Lang	Don Cook	Cheri L. Quinn
John Bell	Elizabeth S. Manera	Sheliah A. Dorton	Shari Smith
Sheri Gannon	Terri St. Michel	Mary Harthune	Kay Terry

We acknowledge the Association of Teacher Educators; their Executive Director, Gloria Chernay; and their presidents—Shirley Robards, Dora Scott-Nichols, John McIntyre, Tom Buttery, and Leonard Kaplan—for supporting this project that is now published by Kappa Delta Pi and its members.

vii

Substitute Teaching:

Planning for Success

ix

Preface

To the Substitute Teacher

Today's job market for K–12 teaching positions is highly competitive, especially among recent college graduates with little classroom experience and those individuals who have been out of the teaching mainstream for years. Substitute teaching has become an avenue for these educators to enter the classroom and gain needed experience before obtaining a full-time contract position. Asked why she was substituting, one college graduate lamented that it was "because I don't have another choice to get into the school system. It seems that you have to be a substitute prior to gaining a permanent teaching position" (St. Michel 1994).

For some, substitute teaching—which appears to mirror regular teaching—provides a good transition. After all, a substitute is required to fulfill the roles and expectations of the classroom teacher in his or her absence, so it would seem that substituting and regular teaching are, in many ways, synonymous.

In some respects, however, a substitute teacher's job is easier than that of the regular classroom teacher. There are often fewer demands and responsibilities. As one substitute noted, "The major preparation, planning, and evaluation remain with the regular classroom teacher. Following the teachers' plans and meeting their expectations are my goals" (St. Michel 1994).

Yet being a substitute is not without its challenges. Indeed, Johnson, Holcombe, and Vance (1988, 89) indicated that "the expectations of substitutes—to teach a class they are not prepared for, to maintain order and discipline in a classroom of students they have never seen before, and to operate in an environment foreign to them—are perhaps greater than the expectations for regular teachers." Because of these extraordinary expectations and demands, substitute teachers must have worthwhile resources and the information necessary to perform their jobs effectively.

Whether it is by choice or by circumstance that you substitute teach or plan to begin, this book offers you that critical information about the substituting process, gathered from educators across the United States at all levels—elementary, middle school, high school, and college. The prologue revealed the wide participation among educators that culminated in this handbook. This book is a proud collaboration among experienced substitute teachers, beginning teachers, master classroom teachers, and teacher educators who all contributed with the goal to provide substitute teachers with a single volume for on-the-job use that gives practical knowledge, management strategies, and supplemental lessons.

The authors are indebted to Terri St. Michel for many of the quotations from substitute teachers found in this book. An English teacher, Dr. St. Michel interviewed dozens of substitutes as she conducted research for her doctoral dissertation. The quotations appear here for the first time in print, even though the content of the many interviews was summarized within her dissertation, listed in the bibliography.

Substitute Teaching offers you:

- steps in obtaining a position as a substitute teacher;

- strategies for managing student behavior;

- forms for needed recordkeeping;

- 30 substantive lesson plans, each written by a practicing teacher;

- short lessons for the start or conclusion of class;

- evaluation forms you can use and share with school districts;

- tips for becoming a successful educational professional; and

xi

- an overview of the rights of teachers and students in today's schools.

Chapter 1 describes who are substitute teachers and the roles and expectations they confront. Beginning in this chapter and throughout the book, the authors refer to the permanent contract teacher whom the substitute replaces as the "regular" teacher. After you read this first chapter, you may assess your preparedness to assume the responsibilities of substituting by matching your qualifications to those identified for successful substituting.

Chapter 2 discusses the steps in obtaining a substitute teaching position. It gives suggestions to help you decide where to apply, how to apply, and what are the key elements of the interviewing process. Chapter 3 provides you with the nuts and bolts of the job of a substitute—preparing before your first assignment, learning classroom logistics, preparing backup lessons, compiling your survival kit, reporting, and recordkeeping—all vital for successful classroom management.

New substitutes identify discipline as the most challenging aspect of being a substitute. Chapter 4 looks at this human relations aspect of the classroom—managing student behavior. You will read about eight different models of discipline and how you can adopt the principles of these models and apply their recommended practices to specific classroom situations.

Chapters 5, 6, and 7 address broadly what substitutes should know when teaching in elementary (K–5), middle (6–8), and high (9–12) schools. While this handbook cannot provide for the special needs of each specific grade level and content area, it does present an overview of the level and what are the developmental behaviors of students at these stages. The handbook also contains 10 lesson plans for each level, complete with teacher instructions and handouts for duplication and distribution to students. While general, each lesson—written by a master teacher—has educational value for students at that level. The lesson format is consistent throughout so it provides you with a model in designing your own lessons for future substituting assignments.

Chapter 8 details how you can determine your success as a substitute teacher. It addresses professionalism, evaluating your performance, and your knowledge of legal issues affecting educational settings. The handbook ends with a glossary of educational terms used throughout the book and an annotated bibliography for further reading.

The authors wish you many happy, fulfilling days as a successful substitute teacher. Enjoy the experience as an opportunity for your own growth as well as to help the students within your charge to do the same. Substitute teaching can be a lot of fun and very rewarding. With a little help, the answers to a few questions, and some experience, you will be a success. We hope that this handbook will become dog-eared from frequent use and encourage you to send your comments and suggestions about *Substitute Teaching* to Kappa Delta Pi Publications, P.O. Box A, West Lafayette, IN 47906-0576.

Good luck!

Chapter 1

The "Substitute"

The substitute teacher is a troubleshooter, manager, creative genius, and reliable pinch-hitter for what happens in today's classroom. Substitute teaching requires the ability to walk into any classroom setting—self-contained, individualized, departmentalized, honors, or specialized—and to carry out daily activities as would the regular—trained and experienced—teacher. In addition to being the "teacher on call"—required to be ready at any moment for a new classroom assignment—substitute teachers are also expected to demonstrate quality in their teaching. Because of these expectations, substitute teaching is one of the most difficult assignments within a school system.

Who Are Substitute Teachers?

What many people conjure when they think of substitute teachers is a stereotype much like the one Trotter and Wragg (1990, 253) describe:

> The stereotypical view of the supply teacher [substitute] is of a female, usually in her thirties, who, after some years teaching, left her permanent job to become a mother. Her children have usually passed the "young baby" stage and can be left with a child-minder. She takes on supply work not only to help the family's finances but for intellectual stimulation and to help her, both emotionally and practically, "get back into teaching."

The reality is quite different. Substitute teachers are men and women who range in age from 18 to 80. Some have a community college education, while others have done extensive postgraduate work. Some substitute part-time, while others earn a full-time living substituting. They are recent college graduates and recent retirees. Many have taught, but others have never been in front of a class. They substitute for a single class period, an entire day, a week, or even a semester. In short, the characteristics of professional substitute teachers are as diverse as those of the students they teach.

1

Do You Qualify to Be a Substitute Teacher?

The expectations for substitute teachers are virtually the same as those for regular teachers. After all, substitutes are "filling in" for regular teachers and are, therefore, taking on the same professional responsibilities and expectations. A teacher once told a sub, "You *are* the teacher. You make the decisions as if this were your classroom."

The degree to which a substitute is expected to follow through on the items listed below depends a great deal upon the length of time that he or she will be replacing the regular teacher. However, it is important for all substitutes to know what may be expected. Thus, substitute teachers may perform some or all of the following when necessary:

- Provide appropriate classroom instruction for the subject and grade level taught. Start by following the regular teacher's lesson plans, and create your own as needed.
- Be responsible for neat, accurate, and complete records and their timely submission. Take roll and lunch count, and turn in a daily attendance roster.
- Maintain the physical appearance of the classroom and care for a variety of equipment. The regular teacher will want to come back and find everything in its place.
- Carry out an assortment of campus duties that may include monitoring students as they get on and off school buses, while eating their lunches in the cafeteria, or as they participate in playground activities. Be ready for anything . . . anywhere . . . anytime.
- Be available for conferences and student make-up

work. You are subbing for the teacher in *all* of his or her roles.

- Complete a progress report form for all students. This will apply particularly to those subbing in a long-term assignment.
- Make telephone calls or home visits as necessary for the welfare of students. Even as a substitute, it can be very important to establish rapport with parents.
- Carry out other duties as stated in school board policies and state statutes. Read the materials that schools and district offices give to you, and comply with all the instructions.
- Prepare lesson plans for subjects with which you are not familiar or for which you have no experience teaching.

This overview of the types of duties school districts may ask of you is not exhaustive, but it should give you a point of reference. The better equipped you are to handle these responsibilities, the easier it will be for you, and the more students will benefit from your expertise. To determine if you *are* equipped to be a successful substitute teacher, you must honestly evaluate whether you possess the key teaching skills, professional attributes, and personal characteristics necessary for this challenging position.

Key Teaching Skills

With instructional time at a premium, substitute teachers must perform with the same artistry as regular teachers to keep students involved in worthwhile activities and motivated to participate fully. Some key teaching skills include knowledge of content, skills in planning and classroom management techniques, and the ability to establish and maintain rapport. More specifically, the substitute teacher should be able to:

- Arouse student interest and enthusiasm;
- Demonstrate knowledge of subject matter (when assigned to areas of your expertise);
- Demonstrate the capability to handle unfamiliar content;
- Keep students focused on the lessons;

Substitute Needed!

Must like children. Must be able to carry out lesson plans. Must be competent to manage a classroom. Must be flexible and spontaneous. Must be willing to work with ambiguity. Must be a "jack-of-all-trades." Must have a keen sense of humor.

Apply within

Join Our Team

Full time carpet cleaner needed in the following areas: Clarksburg, Anderson, Madison and Germantown. Must be a self-starter and willing to work all shifts. For

- Anticipate the time necessary for carrying out activities;
- Allow students the opportunity for appropriate independent and small-group participation;
- Direct activities that give students visual, tactile, and auditory learning experiences;
- Stimulate creative and original thought;
- Provide appropriate reinforcements for positive student behavior;
- Offer alternate choices for those choosing not to behave;
- Recognize varied student abilities and attempt to provide for these differences within the limits of the classroom situation; and
- Set expectations for students' participation and learning.

The most important aspect of substitute teaching is working successfully with students. This requires strong teaching skills and a stronger sense of responsibility for carrying them out. After working for three years in an inner-city school, one veteran substitute (St. Michel 1994) said:

> I have found a new level of self-assuredness as a substitute. I love the kids, and I am challenged with the chance to work with high-risk kids and celebrate their victories in learning, no matter how small. When the kids are happy, I'm happy. I am challenged with keeping them on task when the teacher is out.

A substitute teacher adapts to various subject areas, students, and lessons to maximize the learning time for students.

Professional Attributes

Effective substitute teachers demonstrate a professional attitude both in and out of the classroom. They know what it takes to gain the respect of administrators, regular teachers, and, most importantly, students. Administrators frequently request and often hire these substitutes for permanent teaching positions. Professional substitutes:

- Respect the personal worth of each student;
- Encourage lifelong learning;
- Honor confidences;

- Adhere to established school policies and procedures;
- Promote positive self-esteem and self-concept in all students;
- Promote fair treatment and positive behavior;
- Help students recognize their academic successes and special problem areas; and
- Respond favorably to supervision and suggestions for improvement.

Substitutes who exhibit these attributes have integrity and value the work they do. One substitute noted (St. Michel 1994) that subbing

> is an opportunity to connect and interact with students in a meaningful way. It gives me a chance to experience what goes on in other classrooms, thus helping me to have a more complete, broader understanding of other teachers' and students' situations.

Personal Characteristics

The fine line between professional attributes and personal characteristics might point to why some individuals are more successful than others at substitute teaching. Who you are influences how you operate in the classroom, how you carry out your responsibilities, and how you react to difficult situations. Substitutes should:

- Act consistently in handling students;
- Have an enthusiastic and understanding disposition;
- Enjoy the challenge of varied teaching assignments;
- Manage routine efficiently;
- Maintain a friendly and positive public-relations posture;
- Respond in a sensitive manner to student needs;
- Be dependable, punctual, poised, self-controlled, patient, and tactful;
- Display a sense of humor; and
- Dress professionally.

Perhaps the best substitute teachers are those who are self-starters, who take the initiative, who are self-reflective, and who have the energy to meet the demands of this complex job. Substitute teaching, while formidable, brings unexpected rewards, challenges, and growth.

3

Chapter 2

Securing a Substitute Teaching Position

I want to substitute because I love connecting and interacting with students. In addition, I value the learning opportunities subbing affords me. Finally, it gives me a chance to experience what goes on in other classrooms, thus helping me to have a more complete, broader understanding of other teachers' and students' situations.

—Anonymous (St. Michel 1994)

Once you have decided to become a substitute teacher, your next challenge is to secure a position. Remember that you must first get a valid teaching certificate from your state department of education for any position you are seeking. Many of the steps you will take toward being hired as a substitute are similar to those required for locating and landing a permanent teaching position. In most situations, getting a job as a substitute teacher is rather easy; the demanding part comes when you receive the first telephone call with an assignment. Then you will be held accountable for fulfilling the expectations of administrators, regular classroom teachers, and students. However, while you are replacing the regular classroom teacher, your responsibilities are different, requiring some very special skills and an understanding of the critical role you will play.

The process of securing a position varies greatly from school district to school district and from state to state. Basically, there are four primary areas that are common to the employment search. They are: (1) deciding where to work; (2) applying for the job; (3) interviewing with administration; and (4) following up to ensure serious consideration for a position.

Where Should You Teach?

Your first decision should be to determine the school districts and schools in which you would like to teach. If you are unfamiliar with your local community, contact your State Department of Education (call directory assistance in your state's capital) and request contact information for all school districts along with a map of the state, outlining the location of each district. Use this information to generate a list of target districts.

Preparing a brief list of screening questions that address your professional and personal considerations about teaching can help you narrow your choices from those schools and districts on your list. By calling the personnel office of each district, you can then evaluate the school using your criteria or issues and decide which schools are of most interest to you. Consider asking questions such as these:

- What are the requirements for applicants for substitute teaching positions?
- How do I apply for a substitute teaching position in your school or district?
- How often can I expect to substitute?
- Are there restrictions against being an active substitute in two or more school districts simultaneously?
- What other regulations or restrictions concerning substitute teachers exist in your school or district?
- What are the key characteristics of the school—urban, rural, gifted, magnet, etc.?
- What transportation concerns will I have if I work at your school?
- Who will be contacting me with assignments (e.g., principal, secretary)? What time are the calls generally made?
- What is the daily pay rate?

How Do You Apply for the Position?

Once you have decided which districts meet your criteria, the next step is to request that each district mail an application to you. You may, instead, stop by the district offices to obtain one. When filling out your application, be sure to type in all requested information neatly, being thorough and careful to complete all sections. This is one of the most crucial components of the hiring process. It is the first impression you'll make!

In addition to completing the paperwork, you may also have to:

- Supply letters of recommendation, character references, fingerprints, and official transcripts.
- Present *copies* of your driver's license, social security card, and teaching or substituting certificates.
- Sign an oath of office.
- Fill out other forms as required by the school district.

In order to demonstrate your literacy skills, knowledge, and experience, you may also be asked to write an essay related to substituting or teaching in general. Therefore, you may want to practice answering such typical applicant essay questions as these:

- As a substitute teacher, what is your most important job?
- As a substitute teacher, how would you handle a disruptive student?
- Why do you want to be a substitute teacher in this district (or this school)?

How Do You Prepare to Interview?

What should you expect during the interview? The interviewer is looking for someone to replace the regular classroom teacher competently—someone who can step into unfamiliar environments, take charge, and make things happen. Your confidence and competence will help you land that job. Remember, you are a professional. The interviewer is also a professional—he or she may be a school principal or from the district personnel office. The impression you make is key to securing the position. Consider all aspects of the interview.

What Should You Wear?

Look your best. Wear something tailored, clean, and pressed. Remember, you will be judged on how you look and how you present yourself.

What Should You Say?

Answer questions directly. Offer brief explanations or examples. You will usually have about three minutes in which to answer each question. Be succinct, yet give enough information to satisfy your audience. Refrain from tangential comments or "stories." Common interview questions may include:

- What is your teaching experience?
- Why do you want to substitute teach?
- What are your long-term career goals?
- What do you hope to gain from substituting?
- What do you know about this district or school?
- Are you willing to substitute in any content area and at any grade level?
- Are you willing to substitute on any day of the week, at any school in the district?
- What would you do if a teacher has not left lesson plans?
- How would you describe your classroom management style?

What Should You Do?

Shake hands when you are introduced. Maintain eye contact with the interviewer and speak clearly. At the end of the interview, thank the interviewer for his or her time. Good manners and a little graciousness go a long way! If you have a portfolio of your work, take it along to share with the interviewer. The ideal portfolio will include curricular units you have developed, sample lesson plans, letters of recommendation, certificates of recognition, or other tangible evidence of your experience. You might want to compose a file folder for the interviewer that contains photocopies of some key portfolio documents.

What Should You Ask?

Most of the time interviewers will give you the opportunity to ask questions at the end of the interview. It is important to ask a few questions to indicate a genuine interest, to clarify your understanding, and to provide feedback or insight. However, be careful not to ask too many questions or to ramble. Limit yourself to two or three carefully considered questions and, if necessary, prepare these in advance. Some sample questions you may wish to include are:

- Does the school or district have some type of substitute training program?
- Do teachers assume extra duties that substitutes

are expected to assume?
- Are substitutes expected to attend faculty meetings?
- Do you want me to make a direct contact with the teacher for whom I will be substituting?
- What are the district discipline policies and procedures?

What Follow-up Is Important?

What should you do to follow up the interview? The personal touch can be very effective. Within a few days of your meeting, write a thank-you note to the interviewer. Call the office where you interviewed to confirm the spelling of the interviewer's name and title, and check whether you have been placed on the district's substitute list. Ask when you might expect to receive further information or to obtain substitute materials, such as the district's policies and procedures, and a substitute's manual, if available. When you know which campuses you'll be serving, visit them. Request campus maps and bell schedules. Be proactive, and show your interest in the district, but use discretion and do not make a pest of yourself.

How Do You Maintain Your Position?

Substitute teachers are responsible for fulfilling the expectations of administrators, regular classroom teachers, and students in order to ensure instructional continuity. Knowing and understanding these expectations can serve as a guide for the way you operate. In short, if you know what you are supposed to do, you have a better chance of doing it effectively and efficiently.

Freedman (1975, 96) said, "From the school administrator's point of view, the substitute replaces the regular teacher with as little break in routine as possible." Ultimately, administrators want substitutes to arrive on time, be in classrooms on time, take accurate attendance, maintain order, and willingly fulfill other duties as assigned—monitoring the playground, cafeteria, or bus area; attending assemblies; and working in tutoring and/or computer labs. An administrator's primary concern is that there are no "problems" with the substitute or his or her interactions with students.

Regular classroom teachers have five basic expectations of substitutes. These are to:

- Take attendance;
- Follow the lesson plans provided;
- Keep students on task and engaged in the assigned activities;
- Maintain the physical order of the classroom; and
- Leave a note describing what the substitute and students accomplished, how the students behaved, and what else may have occurred that was not part of the regular classroom teacher's plan.

If no lesson plans have been left and you must create your own, initially check the generic lesson plans found in Chapters 5, 6, and 7 of this book. Leave copies of the lesson plans and activities (or a thorough description of what you did during the school day) for the regular classroom teacher. Politely explain that you found no lesson plans.

If lesson plans are available, complete each part as thoroughly as you can. Describe specifically any unexpected interferences that prevented you from carrying out the regular classroom teacher's plans, such as a fire drill. If possible, contact the regular teacher the day before you will substitute to review the lesson plans and to receive any needed clarification. A substitute (St. Michel 1994) stated, "I have substituted in many classes where teachers left excellent lesson plans, which made my activities a part of the ongoing greater plan for the education of the class. I was actually *expected* to teach as if this were my own class."

Students are a crucial component in making the substitute's day a success. Therefore, you must quickly establish rapport and set the tone if you want to elicit cooperation from students. Students expect substitutes to take charge and to know what they're doing. When asked what they thought substitutes should do, a group of students said (St. Michel 1994):

- They should be able to teach the class and not baby-sit;
- As soon as the students have entered the classroom, subs should introduce themselves and get a good start with the students; and
- They should get involved with the students, be on time, and know what they are doing.

Landing a position means you have successfully completed the paperwork and the interviewing process, satisfying the criteria of the school or district's administration. Maintaining a successful position as a substitute teacher requires your expertise in knowing and carrying out the expectations of the stakeholders—administrators, teachers, and students. Remember that being flexible and dependable, having a friendly yet firm disposition, and a desire to work with students will help ensure that you are at the top of the district's substitute list and are called back as often as you care to work.

7

ENTER THE ROOM WITH CONFIDENCE... LOOK EVERY STUDENT DIRECTLY IN THE EYE AS YOU SPEAK TO HIM OR HER...

Managing the Role

The first time I was called for a substituting position I thought I was as well prepared as most. I was a junior in college, I had always made good grades in school, and I was sure that I could handle any situation that might arise, for you see, I was an education major. But at the end of that day, I dragged myself home to my husband and child to reflect on the day and to figure out what had happened. Maybe it was the student who was moving halfway around the world and needed a grade in that class before she could check out of school. Or it could have been the student who threw his books out of the second-story window and then had to leave class to retrieve them. Then there was the student who came into class pulling a string that supposedly was attached to his pet dog. This was a challenge as he repeatedly reached down to speak to the dog and pet it during class. But I think one of the biggest problems was that they were doing things that I remembered doing or laughing about just a few years before. But now I was on the other side of the desk, and it felt *very* different. Was I too young to substitute? Was I not stern enough in my manner? Had I forgotten to do something? Was I unprofessional? My answer was easy to see but not easy to accept. If I had just planned ahead, my comfort level with the tasks ahead would have been greatly improved, and I wouldn't have left school that day wondering if I still wanted to be a teacher.

—Anonymous substitute teacher (St. Michel 1994)

What Are the Nuts and Bolts of School and Classroom Logistics?

The substitute in this illustration asks some very good questions that you may wish to ask yourself before you go any further with your plan to substitute teach. Self-confidence is certainly important, but it must include a sound foundation of information and technical skills to be able to accomplish the job. Walking into a classroom with a plan to "wing it" because it appears so easy or just letting the students direct you from one activity to the next because they know the routine better than you may get you in trouble.

If you have never done any substituting, this chapter will provide you with a number of suggestions to help make your first experience a successful one. If you are an "old hand" at substituting, perhaps you can add some new ideas to your file.

Before Your First Assignment

Your application to substitute has been accepted; your name has been placed on the substitute roster. Now the real work begins. When you applied and interviewed, you gained only the information about the district that you needed for those hiring processes. However, you must now prepare for the first day on the job by gathering as much information as is available. If you are quite familiar with the schools, your data-gathering will be simple. If, on the other hand, you do not know the area, the first task is to seek additional information about the district and school in which you will be teaching.

Gather as Much Information as Possible. If you only spoke to someone at the district personnel office, you may wish to make an appointment to visit each school where you hope to substitute. When visiting the school, try to speak with the principal or assistant principal about your desire to substitute and your availability. Leave your name, address, and phone number with the school secretary. A business card provides a quick and professional way to give schools the needed information for future assignments. If there is no district orientation for substitute teachers, request copies of the teacher handbook, student handbook, substitute guidelines, and a map of the school. Because you must become familiar with the school facilities, request a tour. This will enable you to find your way around when you return as a substitute. Make notes on the school map to assist you on that first day.

Some districts have developed substitute teacher handbooks and training sessions to prepare substitutes for their schools. Be certain to get school and district calendars for the current year, especially if you have applied to more than one district. When reviewing a

calendar, note the exact dates that school is closed for vacations such as Thanksgiving, winter break, and spring break. These can be high employment times for you, as teachers sometimes use their personal days during these seasons. Other high-employment opportunities include the flu and cold season in January, February, and March, and the right-before-school-gets-out "hair-pulling" days of May. Many districts close the schools for professional development days and permit substitutes to attend. Take advantage of opportunities to be a part of the in-service or, if the schools are open, be ready to replace a teacher who is attending.

If you are unfamiliar with the district, take note of the directions to each school or draw yourself a map showing each school's location. Organize the information about each school in its own folder for easy access. Include any notes you have made about the school. When the phone rings early in the morning—or at any time of day—you will be able to pull out a collection of material about that particular school and review quickly as you prepare to leave. Other details you may wish to include in each school's folder concern the:

- Parking situation;
- Time the building opens (so you won't waste time being too early);
- Person to report to when arriving on campus;
- Procedure for checking in and out of campus;
- Room key policy;
- Normal lesson plan location;
- Teacher instructions for the substitute;
- Attendance procedure;
- Emergency contacts and procedures (fire, tornado, earthquake);
- Lunch procedures for students;
- Lunch arrangements for teachers, including cost;
- Nonteaching duties for substitutes (hall duty, bus duty, study hall supervision, playground or commons area duty, lunchroom duty, etc.);
- Dates of pay (may be different for substitutes, and different from district to district); and
- Daily pay for substitutes, including half-day pay (keep good records because mistakes may be made).

If you have not been able to acquire all the data previously suggested, be prepared to get this information from the person calling you or from the person to whom you report at the school. Being prepared with as much information as possible will improve your chances for a successful day.

Receiving Assignments. Districts have a variety of ways to hire substitutes. Large districts frequently have central calling systems through which the entire district may contact substitute teachers. Some systems are computerized, while others have a single person who handles it all, taking calls from teachers and contacting the substitutes. Schools in other districts each handle their own substitutes. Find out how each school handles hiring so you will understand the procedure and know the name and phone number of the person to whom you report. The person who calls you is probably the most important person to know—and upon whom you must make an especially good impression. If you turn down opportunities to substitute very often, you may find that you will not be called again. Whether or not you are called may depend upon this individual and the comments that he or she receives about your work.

Your First Day of Substituting

If you are called in time to do so, arrive early the first morning so that you can check in with time to spare. Walk around the school to find the restrooms (student and faculty), gym, library, cafeteria, and the "special" classrooms where students may go during the day. When you check in at the office, be sure to obtain any necessary materials that you may need. Because the principal, assistant principal, and school secretary tend to be very busy just prior to the start of morning classes, they will *not* have time to talk with you at length. However, if you were not told any of the following information when you were called, find out (1) if there is a special class (e.g., art) scheduled for that day; (2) where the teacher's lesson plans are; (3) where to find the equipment or materials needed to complete the lesson plan; and (4) if the teacher had any special responsibilities outside of the classroom that you will be expected to assume. You could clarify these items with neighboring teachers if the office is busy, but you *must* do so before the students arrive.

If a tour of the school was not available before your first day, or if you are running a bit late, refer to the map for the location of your classroom, and quickly familiarize yourself with other important places in the building. Be aware that some schools lock faculty restrooms—especially in the middle schools and high schools—so you will need to find out how to gain access to them. You may also want to locate the teachers' lounge, especially if that is where teachers eat lunch. It is usually not a good idea to spend too much time in the lounge. Your time is better spent in the classroom, familiarizing yourself with the day's plans, teaching materials, and other needs. The picture of a busy substitute gives a better impression of you and your professional ability.

Class Information You Need

When you are comfortable with the logistics, make sure that you locate necessary materials in the classroom for the day's plans. Try to find the following items on, in, or near the teacher's desk or podium:

- Substitute information or directions left by the teacher;
- Regular class schedule and special days schedule;
- Lesson plans or plan book;
- Grade book;
- Attendance forms;
- Seating chart(s);
- Textbooks, teacher manuals, workbooks;
- Worksheets, materials, and visuals needed for the planned lesson;
- Classroom procedure and rules; and
- Tornado, fire, earthquake, or other emergency procedures and exits (may be posted by door).

More districts and schools are requiring teachers to have substitute teacher files with updated information in their classrooms or on file in the school office. These may be kept on the desk or in a drawer for easy access along with seating charts, a copy of class rolls, and lists of students who go to special activities or classes.

Your Survival Kit

One way to be well prepared for all eventualities is to develop a "survival kit" to carry with you. Your kit will vary according to what grade levels and subjects you will be teaching. This kit should contain a variety of materials you do not wish to be without and those that supplement what the regular teacher may leave for you. Select items from the list below that are appropriate for the day's specific assignment and slip them into a small bag. The kit might include:

- this handbook;
- blank paper, both unlined and lined;
- blank transparencies;
- transparency markers or water-soluble pens;
- a selection of pencils, pens, markers, and crayons;
- lesson plans (Chapters 5, 6, and 7 of this Handbook contain plans for 10 content areas at the elementary, middle school, and high school levels; or use your own successful plans);
- a selection of books and short stories suitable for the grades you are teaching (everyone likes to be read to);
- scissors, glue, ruler, tape, thumbtacks, rubber bands, Post-it™ notes, small stapler;
- quick and easy activities that you can use to become familiar with the students and the room (see suggested sponge starter activities listed on pages 15–17);
- prepare a short activity that can be completed at the beginning of class while you're taking attendance (refer to The First Five Minutes found on page 17);
- select a 10-minute discussion topic from page 18 or a short supplemental activity from pages 19–20 when there is time left in the day;
- a whistle for gym or recess;
- money for lunch; and/or
- change for the soft-drink machine and the pay phone.

What Management Techniques Will Help You Succeed?

To be a good substitute teacher, you must be able to manage a classroom filled with unfamiliar, highly diverse, and sometimes disruptive students. A typical day will begin with you alone, in front of a classroom, as the only "outsider." Regardless of any ambivalent feelings you may have about your situation, remember that you are in charge and have the responsibility and authority to teach this class!

Develop an Attitude

Be assertive and confident on the outside, regardless of your inner feelings. Despite how unfair it may seem, the class will remember you based on the first impression that you give them. You only have one chance to make a first impression—be approachable, friendly, fair, and firm.

Enter the room with an air of confidence that you may or may not feel. Look everybody—students and colleagues alike—directly in the eye as you speak to him or her, and begin to set your pace for a business-like, work-oriented day. With your new attitude solidly in place, you have a good start on gaining the students' attention and respect.

Learn the School Discipline Plan

If you receive substitute materials from the district or school office, there should be a reference to the official discipline plan. Locate the listing, and quickly review the basic format of the plan, attempting to relate it to your own philosophy and experience. Because consistency is a key to good discipline, you may want to align yourself as much as possible with that particular school's accepted practice. Next, search through the materials left by the regular teacher to find anything that may relate specifically to the discipline policies in your assigned classroom. Often the classroom rules or standards will be posted in an elementary or middle school classroom.

Seek Assistance

You may find that you need some quick answers. You could ask a neighboring teacher—or turn to one of the real experts on this class, a helpful student. Many teachers will leave the names of trustworthy students, or you could ask a neighboring teacher to suggest the name of a student who might be helpful. Several students will probably be quite open and helpful regarding, for example, where to find important classroom items or the routine procedures that govern the class. Asking for assistance from a class member is a good springboard for interaction. While there may be some devious answers meant to confuse the situation, ask for specific information and you'll generally be rewarded with quick and correct answers. Throughout the day, other opportunities to build rapport with students will abound. Take advantage of these!

Start with Purpose

Your day of substituting may begin something like this: you gain the attention of the class, introduce yourself, write your name on the board, and immediately give the students—especially in the elementary grades—an introductory activity (also referred to as a sponge activity because it soaks up extra time) to do while you take attendance and do other necessary bookkeeping or housekeeping. Some suggested 5- or 10-minute activities that could be used are listed on pages 15–17. If you take attendance without giving the students something to do, you might lose control of the class before you begin. When you are ready to start the lesson, introduce the topic that the teacher has provided, and the interactive process of teaching begins.

At first, the class might view you as new and interesting. You will be flattered with their attention. However, a student may interject an irrelevant comment, make an inappropriate sound or two, or even engage in a shouting match with another student. Inform the class of your expectations and their responsibilities. Handle each impertinence deftly and efficiently, coolly maintaining your composure. Be constantly in motion, surveying your students' work. It is important for you to be prepared for anything. And know that some days will be easier than others.

Follow the Lesson Plan

The role of the substitute teacher is to pick up where the regular classroom teacher left off the day before. The regular teacher's plan includes a time line or calendar for coverage of the subject matter. To maintain this schedule, the substitute must complete the day's assignments as much as possible.

As you are introducing yourself and establishing your teaching and learning environment, you may refer to the teaching plan. If you are fortunate, the plan will be a complete lesson that includes how to present the

lesson, what textbooks to use, what papers to distribute and collect, and which papers to grade and record. If you are less fortunate, it could be a rather sketchy plan, such as the one that was once left for a kindergarten class. It simply read, "Blow up balloons"—not much to go on. You must then hastily pull something together or provide supplemental, but related, material that you feel your expertise can handle.

To allow for a smooth transition from introductory matters to the business of learning, your plan should be close at hand and ready to use. If the teacher has left no plans, you should have a lesson of your own ready. The lesson activities found in Chapters 5, 6, and 7 of this handbook are there for just such situations. However, if you wish to create your own, make the lesson worthwhile and consistent with the learning environment you are creating in your focused and disciplined classroom.

Regardless of the situation you inherit, it is up to you to make the plan work. Handling unfamiliar content may be a challenge to you. Look for skills, concepts, or processes that are similar to those in familiar content and that cut across content boundaries. Then ask students to select the important points they are studying and to summarize major learning, either in writing or orally. You could ask students to teach you about what they have been learning (developing summarization and review skills as well as motivation) and build from there.

Put Everything in Its Place

As you progress through the day, continually assess the condition of the room. Periodically, ask the students to help pick up and put things back in order. If the students see you straightening the classroom without their assistance, they might decide that it is fun to make a bigger mess for you to clean up. You must foresee possible situations like this and plan ahead so that they will not occur.

As you prepare to leave, check the room to be sure that it is neat and clean. Be sure there is no paper on the floor, desks are arranged in the same configuration as they were when you arrived in the morning, chalk-

12

boards are erased, and equipment is put away. Leave the room the way you would expect to find it if you were the regular classroom teacher.

Custodians are influential. Make their job as easy as possible—and ensure yourself of their appreciation. If you have any questions about classroom maintenance, the custodian will usually be happy to answer them.

How Should You Report on Classroom Activities?

Each school or district has specific forms for recordkeeping with which the substitute teacher should be familiar. Sometimes there is a substitute teacher orientation workshop or meeting where substitutes are provided copies of the forms and given information on how to maintain them. However, if this is not true in your case, it is imperative that you find out about the forms. Do not be afraid to ask questions. The clearer the procedures and the more detailed the directions you receive, the smoother your time in the classroom will be. For example, attendance is taken by virtually every school, but each has a different method for handling it. Many schools use a computer attendance program of some kind, while other schools have slips of paper on which the teacher writes the names of absent students. Find out what forms—including those for attendance, lunch money collection, hall passes, etc.—should be used and the process for completing each. Whether you use the forms developed by the school or ones that you make up on the spot, be sure to follow through carefully. If you are reporting a classroom incident, be sure to do so accurately, clearly, concisely, and with as much objectivity as possible. Correct details may be very important not only for the teacher, but also for the assistant principal, the principal, and the parents striving to understand the incident and to work through the situation.

Daily Records

Recordkeeping is an important part of a teacher's duties. Accurate records are helpful to the teacher, the school administrator, and the parents. However, most teachers will only have you deal with the daily, routine records. This is particularly true if the regular teacher is only going to be out of the classroom for one day.

Therefore, normally you will only have to take student attendance, count lunch money for elementary students, and provide grades (if applicable) for work that you have assigned. If the students are having special competitions, such as magazine sales, recycling products, or candy sales, they frequently can handle it with your help, or can wait until the regular teacher returns. Make sure that reports are delivered promptly and to the correct person or location.

Attendance

Attendance will normally be your first duty of the day. The regular classroom teacher will need to know if anyone has been absent in order to ensure safety and to give the student an opportunity to make up any work. These records should be clear, accurate, and up-to-date. Record and submit the attendance according to the administration's procedures.

Grading Papers

Sometimes the regular teacher prefers to grade the student's papers so that consistency is maintained. However, if the teacher requests that you evaluate any of the papers, it would be appropriate for you to do so if you have time. Do grade assignments you made that were *not* in the teacher's plans. Be sure to attach a note explaining what you have or have not completed. Also, do not write in the teacher's official records (e.g., grade book) unless directed to do so, but do keep a record of grades and attendance on a separate piece of paper for the teacher to use when he or she returns.

Personal Records

Make a record sheet (use the blank paper in your survival kit) to list attendance, lunch count, lunch money collected, other money collected, homework turned in, anecdotal records, etc., in case no such sheets are provided for your use. It is always good to be prepared "just in case."

Activities Summary

You may find it helpful to record classroom happenings. Include what you did that went well, and identify any problems you had. If you do not have time during the school day, leave room to add to the comments after the school day has ended. Try to decide what you

13

will do differently next time or how you might modify an assignment, directions, or activity.

Day's End

When the school day is over, you will want to place all of the teacher's feedback sheets, the lesson plans, and students' papers on the teacher's desk where he or she can easily find them. All records or materials that you have collected or used during the day should be placed in a folder or clipped together in the correct order. Finally, go to the office to tell them that you are leaving. Return classroom keys, forms, equipment, and other material that you obtained from the office staff.

Feedback

Teachers must know what occurred in their absence. Most teachers wish to know about any problems the substitute teacher had so that they can follow up on them. Therefore, it is most important to provide feedback to the regular teacher in a narrative or a previously developed form. Models are included on pages 21–22 for both elementary and high school teachers.

Some schools ask the regular classroom teachers to evaluate the substitute teacher's performance. If so, you may wish to request a copy. If no such form is used, or a copy is not available, you might develop your own and leave it with a self-addressed, stamped envelope, asking that the teacher evaluate your work and send you the requested input.

What Personal Records Should You Keep?

It is important for you to keep a record of the places you have been substituting and how each assignment went. Keep an assignment log that includes the information in the sample at the bottom of this page.

Reflect upon what went well and what you would like to do differently next time. You might write a narrative about your day's activities using a diary format. Include successful strategies that you wish to repeat and possible suggestions for what can be improved. A self-evaluation form, such as the one on page 135, might be used instead of the assignment log or narrative. It could provide a checklist of behaviors and could end with some unfinished sentences for you to complete (see more about self-evaluation in Chapter 8, pages 132–46). Add any general data about the assignment that you would like to remember the next time you substitute teach in the same school or classroom.

When you begin substituting, accept that you will probably make mistakes. Some classes and some schools are more difficult assignments than others. As you work through these challenges, you will find techniques that work for you and with which you are comfortable. This chapter has given you some of the basics so that you can approach your first few days of substitute teaching with some helpful ideas and strategies. Like becoming a good regular classroom teacher, becoming a good substitute teacher takes time and much hard work. Once you are familiar with the nuts and bolts of the job, the rest is up to you.

14

Date	School	Contact Person	Teacher	Course/Grade	Notes

Story Problems. (grades 2–8) Write a story problem on the chalkboard or overhead that contains unnecessary information. Ask students to copy it, leaving out the unneeded material. They should write a number sentence for the problem and solve it.

Memory. (grades 2–12) Ask students to study a poster (brought in your survival kit) that contains many elements. After three minutes of study, ask the students to quietly and individually list all the items they saw in the poster.

Word Search. (grades 2–12) If the school or you have a computer with the proper software, create a word-search puzzle with vocabulary words, states and capitals, geographic features of your state, parts of the body, U.S. Presidents, U.S. rivers, etc.

Geometry Everywhere. (grades 3–10) Ask students to count off in threes. In five minutes have each group list items in the classroom that match a geometric shape: ones are circles; twos are rectangles; and threes are triangles. They cannot leave their seats to check but must observe from their position.

Mental Math. (grades 2–10) Distribute to each student a 3x5-inch card with a basic math problem. Ask the students to solve the problem mentally without the use of pencils and raise their hands when they have the answer. Be certain that any division steps equal whole numbers. Example:

> 3 plus 5 equals
>
> divided by 2 equals
>
> times 4 equals
>
> minus 1 equals

Alphabetizing. (grades 2–8) List 10–15 words on the board. Ask students to copy each on a sheet of paper, arranging them in alphabetical order.

Imagining. (grades 1–6) Ask students to write a 50-word description of what they would do if they found an elephant, new car, swimming pool, puppy, motorcycle, volleyball net, or disc jockey in their backyard when they returned home from school today.

Communicating. (grades K–12) Ask students to turn to their neighbors and the older of the two should tell the other an interesting experience he or she had within the past three days. The listener must be prepared to summarize the experience in 25 words or less and then share it with the class when you are ready to start.

Estimating. (grades K–12) Give each student a small bag of M&M's (brought in your survival kit). Have the students guess the number of M&M's in the bag and how the colors are distributed. Have them open the bag, and before they eat them, record the number of each color. Older students can graph the results and then compare to obtain an average for the class.

Sponge Starter

Sponge Starter

Writing Poetry. (grades 2–8) Write an alphabet letter on the board. Ask students within two minutes to write as many words as they can that begin with that letter. Then they must use at least five of these words to write a poem.

Getting Acquainted. (grades 2–9) Ask students to print their first and last names vertically down the left margin of a sheet of paper. Then, using each letter as a starting point, have students write adjectives or words representing the special interests that describe them.

What Do You Wanna Know? (grades 2–12) Ask students to write at least three questions they would like answered about events happening in their school, city, or country. After each they should list where they should go or to whom they must talk in order to find the answer.

Who Is She? (grades 4–12) Write vertically on the board the letters in the name: Mrs. N. I. Creed. Tell students that remembering this name will help them remember the 10 systems in the human body. Ask a volunteer to come to the board to write in one system: **M**uscular; **R**espiratory; **S**keletal; **N**ervous; **I**ntegumentary; **C**irculatory; **R**eproductive; **E**xcretory; **E**ndocrine; **D**igestive.

What Does It Mean? (grades 1–12) Distribute copies of a poem suitable for the grade level (brought in your survival kit). Ask students to read the poem and be ready to express the main message of the poet.

What Doesn't Fit? (grades 2–8) Display several arrangements of four words, numbering each arrangement. Ask students to write on a sheet of paper which word does not fit with the other words, and why.

hot soft	pitcher shortstop	president queen
sweet rough	catcher linebacker	mayor prime minister

Series. (grades 4–10) Write several ordered pairs of numbers on the board (e.g., 8, 64; 3, 9; 6, 36) to establish a pattern. Then give only one number at the end of each series and ask the students to list the next number in each series according to its pattern.

General

You can develop rapport with students quickly and efficiently by immediately engaging them in an activity that will also help you learn their names. Before the students come into the classroom, write on the board three questions to elicit what you would like to know about each student, such as "How do you spend most of your time when you are not in school?" "What do you like best about school? math? Spanish? art?" "What three words would your best friend (parents, teacher) use to describe you?" As each student enters the room, give him or her a 3x5-inch card. Ask students to count off in their seated rows and write their numbers in the top right corner of their cards. They should write their names on the top line. Ask them to answer the three questions within four minutes. As you move around the classroom, make positive comments to the students to develop rapport. Based on their level of cooperation and behavior, either ask them to bring their cards to you or raise their hands and you will pick up their cards when they finish. Take attendance as they turn in the cards.

First 5 Minutes

17

10-Minute Topics

If you could have one thing that you really wanted, what would it be? How would it change your life?

Whom do you admire the most, and why?

What did you do lately that made someone happy?

What can you tell me about your school that you think I don't know?

Grades K–3

What person in your life makes you laugh the hardest?

If you could be given more strength, what would you do with it?

What game always makes you fight with someone? Why?

If you are shy, what can you do to make a friend?

Grades 4–6

What do you do that makes you proud of yourself?

If you could be given more courage, what would you do with it?

What did you do last summer that you would love to do again?

If you could go anywhere in the world, where would you choose, and why?

Grades 7–9

What motivates you to try your hardest in school?

If you could be given more confidence, what would you do with it?

If you could teach everyone in the world one thing, what would it be?

What makes a good friend? What evidence can you show that you are a good friend?

Grades 10–12

If you could be given more talent, what would you do with it?

What would you like the student council to do for the students this year?

What do you value the most in your relationships with friends?

What do winning athletic teams do for your school pride?

18

Short Supplemental Activities

Dismissal. Dismiss students by having them say a word that fits a broad category: fruits, U.S. presidents, flowers, colors, two-syllable words, states, animals, world nations, etc.

Listening to Follow Directions. (grades K–4) Depending on the age and maturity level, state several directions in numerical order. Then ask children to follow each direction after you call out each number. Some classes have reached up to 12 directions. Example:

1. Stand up.
2. Put both hands on your head.
3. Turn around.
4. Clap hands twice.
5. Snap fingers once.
6. Sit down.
7. Put head down on desk.
8. Close eyes.

Making Connections. (grades 3–12) Ask students to write down the left margin of a sheet of paper the letters of the alphabet. Ask students to list a word for each letter that relates to the discussion you had earlier in class. Or ask them to think of a long word for each letter, one that has as many letters as possible.

Critiquing the Critic. (grades 5–12) Give the students a newpaper review of a recent movie of interest to this age group. Ask students to write a short essay of 100 words in response to the review. If they have seen the movie, they should write their own review of the movie or react to the opinions expressed by the newspaper writer. If they have not seen the movie, they should describe whether they would go to the movie based on the critic's review, explaining their reasons why or why not.

Dressing the Part. (grades 2–8) Divide the students into teams of 3. Give each team a stack of newspapers and a roll of masking tape. Ask the students to create with their supplies (and no other materials) a costume for one of the team members who will portray a famous person in history (U.S. or world). The team cannot verbally divulge any clues about the figure. Other teams guess the identity of each figure; if necessary, the figure can strike a typical posture for the character.

Describing Culture. (grades 4–12) Place a set of common-day items on a table in the front of the room (brought in your survival kit). The items must together represent a particular culture—modern United States, early colonial era, Native American, or local, for example. Ask students to write a 100-word (or longer) description of what life was like for the people who used these "artifacts" in their daily lives. Modern U.S. culture items could include a rubber thong, bar of soap, packet of sugar, *TV Guide,* penny, sandwich baggie, cotton swab, etc.

Supplemental Activities

Questions they could consider as they write are: Of what materials are the objects made? How were the objects made—by hand or machine? For what purposes were the objects used? What does the object reveal about the people who used it?

Current Events. (grades 1–12) Distribute to two- or three-person teams copies of recent articles from the local newspaper or a popular magazine (brought in your survival kit) on topics of interest for their age group. Ask each team to read its article and pick out 3–5 key ideas to share with the rest of the class.

Writing Humorous Stories. Read an interesting short story aloud to the class (i.e., *Alexander and the Terrible, Horrible, No Good, Very Bad Day*). Have students brainstorm their own list of "Bad Day" events. Students can then write "Bad Day" stories. The emphasis should be on humor. Have students work in pairs and edit stories. Finally, have students read their stories aloud to the class.

Writing Musical Poems. Have students list five song lyrics. Arrange students in groups of three. Students are to put their lyrics together and write a poem. Remind students NOT to use rhyme and to make sure their poem looks like a poem. They are to strive for meaning and theme. Poems can be read aloud to the class.

Parlez-vous Français? Using a cassette tape recorder, record students introducing each other, describing a partner using foreign-language vocabulary they have learned, describing objects in the classroom, etc. The cassette tape can then be left for the regular teacher.

Keeping Up with Current Events. Arrange students in groups of three. Give each group a current article. Have the group summarize the important points of the article. Have the group write its responses that support or refute the article's points. Have each group share its responses to its article.

Measuring Practice. Ask the students to estimate the dimension of their arms, a desk, or a notebook. Measure and compare answers. Make bar graphs to illustrate the results.

Mapping Class. Make a scaled map of the classroom. Have students estimate various paths taken in the room by various individuals. For example, how many steps would a five-foot male take to go from the front of the room to the back? How many for a three-inch white mouse?

Class Charades. Assign easy pantomimes to individual students (you may want to model this before assigning them to the class). Example: pouring a glass of milk. Glass taken from cupboard, refrigerator door must be opened, carton opened, etc. Emphasis should be on correct order of events. This is excellent as a springboard to writing short shories if order of events is stressed.

Form 3–1   **Today's Report from Your Elementary Substitute Teacher**

Date_____

Substitute's Name _____ for _____ Regular Teacher's Name

Substitute's Address _____

Substitute's Phone _____

School_____Grade(s) _____

Principal _____

Students who were absent _____

Notes from Home (attached) _____

Subjects Taught _____

Classwork Completed:

1. Boardwork

2. Homework Collected

3. Work Checked

4. Story

5. Spelling

6. Reading

7. Language Arts

8. Math

9. Science

10. Social Studies

11. Art

12. Music

13. P.E.

14. Other

Homework Assigned _____

Materials/Supplies Distributed _____

Concerns _____

_____

_____

_____

Today's Report from Your Substitute Teacher

Date_____

Substitute's Name _____for _____ Regular Teacher's Name

Substitute's Address _____

Substitute's Phone _____

School_____Grade(s) _____

Principal _____

Subjects Taught

Today I was able to:

_____ Implement your lesson plan(s) as closely as possible.

_____ Leave you a report of work done.

_____ Maintain normal classroom discipline.

_____ Maintain regular classroom routine.

_____ Collect, check, and process school papers and related work.

_____ Leave your classroom in the condition it was found.

_____ Secure and lock the classroom.

_____ Check your teacher's box for mail, messages, memos, updates, materials, etc.

_____ Complete additional requests such as projects, catchalls, and related.

_____ Distribute to pupils bulletins, flyers, school handouts, and/or other pertinent papers.

Important Messages

Concerns

Chapter 4

Managing Students

When most people mention classroom management they mean discipline. Actually, it encompasses everything that goes on in the classroom. It means class organization, how the desks are arranged—straight lines, semicircle, groups of four, etc.—how the teacher uses the chalkboard, where the class library or instructional materials are located, how the students are grouped for instruction, specific instructional techniques, classroom timing, and classroom routines that the teacher has established for turning in homework, returning graded papers, or reporting student progress. In short, classroom management is everything that the teacher does in the classroom to help students grow in a good learning environment. When student behavior and the teacher's attempts to change student behavior interrupt learning in order to reestablish an environment conducive to learning, the class faces issues of discipline.

Managing student behavior is one of the most difficult tasks you will face as a substitute teacher. You must be prepared to react fairly and firmly in a variety of situations without appearing to be overly authoritarian. You will find that the better you have planned classroom time—the more you keep students busy and move around the classroom—the better student behavior will be.

Does classroom management sound like a tall order? Of course it does, but with some self-examination, solid planning, and a few teacher-tested strategies, success is within your reach. To realize this success, you must be as prepared as possible (within the time you are given) for the grade and subjects you are teaching. This chapter will give you some tools to deal with situations that substitutes commonly encounter.

23

What Must You Know about Discipline?

Good classroom management is the key to preventive discipline. A good substitute teacher must have two discipline plans. One discipline plan is for immediate use, such as handling confrontations with students. The other, long-term discipline plan involves creating a long-range positive learning environment.

Your Immediate Discipline Plan

You must have a few strategies designed to shut down misbehavior as soon as it occurs. Dealing with a problem immediately will allow you to get the incident behind you and move on. Then you may continue with the important business of teaching.

Your Long-Range Discipline Plan

You want the rest of the day, and hopefully any future days, in this school to go well. It is particularly important for you to know that you will have a receptive class waiting for you when you return. You want to build a positive reputation for yourself regarding your ability to help students to learn. Key to long-range planning is the sincere effort to get to know your students. Try to develop rapport with them. Without overdoing it, look for ways to build student confidence and self-esteem. Getting to know your students will allow you to create a classroom climate that is trusting, productive, and positive.

A Look at Some Well-Known Discipline Models

It is important for you to be familiar with a number of approaches to meet the acknowledged number one challenge in any classroom, anywhere—discipline. Only when the class is working with you will you be able to accomplish what you are hired to do and are expected to do—teach!

If you like the feeling of being really prepared with the latest theories, practices, and jargon on discipline, or if you are genuinely interested in adding to your philosophy of discipline, you may want to read about some of the better known approaches or plans. Many are included in the chart on pages 26–27, which briefly describes the model developed by each author, identi-

fying its primary components and some specific techniques within the model. For further reading, check the bibliography in Chapter 9 for specific references of the models.

Who's in Charge Here?

One of the biggest hurdles for a substitute is to establish who is in charge. It is essential that students become actively involved in the lesson as soon as possible so that you do not allow students idle time and possible disruptions never materialize. However, if this is a long-term subbing job, you may wish to take some time to find out about the class rules after you have completed at least one lesson, thereby establishing your authority.

One way to approach this issue is to look for the rules that are posted in the classroom or listed in the student, teacher, and/or substitute handbook. If the rules are specifically for that classroom, frequently students have helped to develop some, if not all, of them. Ask various students in turn to read one rule and explain it to you. Allow additional purposeful comments. While this may take a few minutes, you will have a better understanding of the rules, and the students will have reviewed what is expected of them. If a list is not available, guide the students in developing a list of five or six rules that will govern their behavior for the days you are teaching their class. Allowing students to help develop consequences for misbehavior also allows them to have even more ownership of the whole process, and they will feel a sense of empowerment. You are setting the stage for a successful day because the students know what you expect from them, and you have shown the students what person is in charge without demanding control. Try to predict possible situations like this, and have a management plan that will allow you to conduct class successfully.

What Are Some Effective Techniques and Interventions?

Even if you have started the day right by meeting your class with as much composure and assertiveness as you could muster, the class may sense a bluff (real or imagined) at some point. Here are some substitute scenarios with possible courses of action. Because there are no guarantees in this business, if one intervention is unsuccessful, try another, and keep trying until you find the right approach. None of these approaches is wrong, but one alternative may work better than another, and you may need to try several. You, of course, may have experienced such situations before and have yet another alternative to offer for each scenario.

Excessive Talking

Classroom disruptions are generally not serious and probably the most common situation to occur is for students to talk at inappropriate times. Though most incidents are not serious, student conversations may cause you enough distraction to prevent you from concentrating on the lesson or to review directions for an activity for several students. In addition to being rude, this talking may escalate into a more serious "power struggle" between the student and you, or it may spread to other students in the classroom. The situations described here are typical of those you might encounter while substituting. Identify the solution that you think will solve the problem in the best manner.

The Socializing Group. Your assignment is with a seventh-grade class. You have asked the students to form groups of four or five to discuss solutions to several problems. Groups must report solutions to the whole class during the last 20 minutes of the period. One group is socializing and not preparing for discussion. They are wasting time and becoming a distraction to other groups. You could:

* move around the room, ending up close to their group;
* stand by their group and ask how the assignment is coming along;
* intervene directly with the group to engage in problem solving with them; or
* inform them pleasantly (not sarcastically) that when it is time, their group will be called on first to report.

Attention! The bell rang in your fourth-grade classroom over a minute ago, signaling the beginning of the new period. You are trying to get your class ready for a planned activity, but they are loudly involved in their

own conversations and are ignoring you. The few students who are aware of your attempts to gain control of the class seem to be enjoying your frustration. Once more you ask for their attention, but the majority of the class does not seem to hear you. You could:

* jiggle the light switch off and on, wait for the questioning and attentive looks, then begin when they are quiet;
* without a word, extend your hand above your head with the two-fingered "peace sign." When they are quiet, thank them for recognizing the request for quiet;
* thank them for their kind attention several times, each time lowering your voice a notch. Note if the level of their noise matches yours;
* write the words "No Recess" on the board, then begin to erase one letter at a time as some students begin to cooperate, or as the noise level goes (and stays) down and work is completed (could also be done positively adding letters for more recess or free time); or
* pull out a small bell or whistle, and sound it!

An Unwelcome Duet. You are clarifying pronouns to your freshman English class and can't help but notice that, whenever you speak, a young man in the back of the room maintains a continuous dialogue with his friend. The student's speech perfectly coincides with your own. You locate his name on the seating chart. You could:

* maintain steady and meaningful eye contact with the student, showing that you know what is going on;
* continue your lesson, but move across the room, and teach next to the student's chair;
* use the student's name periodically within the text of your lesson on personal pronouns; or
* ask the class to come up with some examples on their own. When they are engaged in this activity, and at the proper time, give the student an "I-message." I-messages can be very effective because they are comprehensive and to the point. You could say, "[Student's name], when you speak while I am talking to the class, I feel that it makes it difficult

Author	Description	Key Components
Canter	Provides a procedure for assertively expecting students to behave with consequences previously known.	• Set clear limits and logical consequences. • Follow through with previously established consequences. • Provide positive reinforcement for desired behavior. • Address situation and not the student's character. • Must have parent and administrator support.
Dreikurs	Students seek recognition; if they cannot get it in acceptable forms, they will by seeking attention, power, or revenge, or by displaying inadequacy.	• Discipline: teaching students to self-impose limits. • Democratic teachers: students help to determine rules and consequences. • Good behavior brings rewards, poor behavior always brings undesired consequences. • Identify students' mistaken goals, and do not reinforce the resulting behavior. • Encourage students, rather than praise. • All students want to belong.
Ginott	Create a social-emotional environment conducive to learning by sending sane messages and treating students as individuals with feelings and self-esteem needs.	• Send sane messages; react to situations not character; state the facts. • Express anger by describing what they see and how they feel about it. • Invite cooperation rather than demand it. • Accept and acknowledge student's feelings and ask what help is needed. • "Labeling is disabling," causing students to reinforce their views of themselves. • "Correction is Direction," tell what is seen and provide alternatives. • Avoid sarcasm to prevent hurt feelings. • Praise only specific acts without adjectives about the student.
Glasser	Curriculum and classroom environment should meet students' basic needs, and be inviting, comfortable, fun, motivating, and provide a sense of belonging.	• Students control their own behavior; they act the way they choose to act. • Bad choices result in bad behavior, good in good. • Do not accept excuses for poor behavior. • Help students make and learn to make good choices. • Follow all behavior, good or bad, with reasonable consequences. • Establish classroom rules, but only rules that will be enforced.
Jones	Help students maintain self-control with body language, incentives, and help during independent time.	• Use body language to set and enforce specific class rules. • Provide incentives that are specific and desired by the students. • Provide efficient help by being brief, positive, and gone using less than 20 seconds per student.
Kounin	Productive classrooms require good lesson management.	• Ripple Effect: reaction to one student will influence other students' behavior. • With-itness: being aware of what is happening in all parts of the classroom. • Overlapping: being capable of dealing with two situations at once. • Movement Management: lessons flow smoothly from one lesson to next. • Group Focus: keeping students' attention on the same topic at the same time. • Avoid satiation: recognize when enough is enough.
Skinner	Using a systematic application of reinforcement, students' behavior can be molded and shaped following desired and planned guidelines.	• Consequences shape behavior. • Systematic, planned use of rewards can help shape desired behavior. • If a reward does not follow the behavior, it weakens behavior. • Punishment also weakens behavior. • Use constant reinforcement early in the situation. • Later in the situation use occasional reinforcement.
Wong	A teacher can always work to improve regardless of the number of years of teaching experience.	• Have positive expectations for student success. • Have a good classroom management skills. • Design lessons that students can master. • Teacher learns and grows professionally. • Teacher is always open to new ideas.

Specific Techniques

- Follow the five steps to assertive discipline.
- Praise when student is behaving properly and ignore misbehavior.
- "Move in" on the space of one or two students and review class behavior procedures.

- "Freeze technique" for group control.
- Use positive repetition for on-task behavior.
- Outline and instruct specific classroom directions.

- Logical consequences: results must directly relate to the behavior.
- Student decision making: students are responsible for behavior and learning.
- Combine kindness and firmness.

- Set limits from the beginning of class.
- Mean what you say, but keep your demands simple.
- Close an incident, and revive good spirits quickly.
- Give explicit directions.

- Describe what you see and express your feelings.
- Send "I messages," indicating how you feel about the situation.
- Enhance your vocabulary by expressing your anger with words that students vaguely understand but are descriptive and powerful.
- Give students choices with alternatives that are within the acceptable limits.

- Provide opportunities for students to act independently.
- Allow face-saving exits.
- Allow students to help set standards for classroom behavior.
- Focus on solutions.
- Model acceptable behavior.

- Use classroom meetings to organize class: identify and review classroom rules.
- Review classroom behavior, and resulting consequences (both positive and negative).
- Call attention to even the smallest good choice made by a student.
- Focus on behaviors that will help them be successful in society.

- Body posture and carriage communicate authority and strong leadership. Move to position near students who are prone to misbehave.
- Facial expressions convey humor and cannot attack the student. Use eye contact to indicate awareness and control.
- Catch misbehavior early, and deal with it immediately.
- Gestures convey meaning without interrupting the verbal processes.

- Provide genuine incentives that are practical and attainable, have educational value, and reflect approved activities.
- Complete the work, then receive the incentive.
- Be prepared to take action when the incentive does not work. Determine an action that is easy to implement.
- Reward or punish group together; group pressure will enhance everyone's desire for the reward.

- Movement Management requires:
  Pacing: going smoothly from one activity to another.
  Momentum: maintaining a constant speed within the lesson.
  Transition: keeping students' attention on the activities when going from one to another.
  Slowdowns: delays that waste time between lesson activities.

- Group Focus requires:
  Group format: encouraging maximum active student participation while working with the whole group.
  Accountability: every student is responsible for learning all the lesson content.
  Attention: all students are continually focused on the class activity.

- Reward student when you observe desired behavior; hopefully, student repeats behavior as a result.
- Ignore or punish student when he or she displays undesired behavior. If student sees rewarded student's behavior, he or she may choose not to repeat misbehavior.

- Reinforcers or rewards may include: facial expressions, gestures, comments, stickers, free time in class, positive notes home, credit toward homework, or points toward a future larger reward.

Multiple techniques that are found in other models are selected to fit the individual situation.

for me to concentrate on my lesson. Please stop." This message is meant to be for the student alone; it should be spoken to him pleasantly, clearly, and directly.

Talk! Talk! Talk! You are well into your lesson on the Civil War. You note that the level of misbehavior in the form of talking and openly socializing in several areas of the classroom has increased. At first it is minimal, so you ignore it; but now you feel that you must act or the situation could escalate. You might:

- ask one of the offending students a question about your lesson;
- move a particularly talkative student to another part of the room;
- distract an offending student by asking him or her to do some task for you; or
- immediately stop the history lesson, and have students read in the textbook and complete an assignment.

Handling Difficult Students

You are the center of attention today because you are not the regular classroom teacher. Some students will offer you positive attention. However, to a few, you will not be viewed as special at all. You will be recognized as just another authority figure to resent. The slightest attempt at correction may result in a challenge from a difficult student.

If an emotional situation develops, certain students will use any means available to intimidate you or any of the other teachers. Sometimes a hostile action or an emotional confrontation will result from a student seeking revenge. The revengeful action may have nothing to do with the student's personal feelings about you. The probable cause may be an aspect of the student's life entirely removed from you, such as a girlfriend, boyfriend, or a family situation. You just happened to be there when his or her emotions piqued. It is important to remain calm; you may not want to speak immediately. You may take action, but not until after the confrontation has subsided.

First of all, identify the students who may be challenging you and the types of behavior you might expect from them. A challenging or difficult student may be described as one who impedes the regular flow of the classroom climate and activity that you desire as a teacher. Students are judged by teachers to be difficult if they:

- engage in extreme acting-out for the purpose of receiving more than their fair share of attention from the teacher;
- seek to confront you when you ask that they perform academically as other students are expected to do; or
- act out verbally and/or physically.

For various reasons, many children are angry and hurting in schools today. When a student "blows up" over a reasonable request from you, it is extremely important that you remain calm and reasonable as you deal with the incident. It is equally important that you do not allow the situation to escalate. Because you want to do your best for all students and assist them in learning and in building self-esteem, let's examine some extreme scenarios.

The Attention-Seeker. A third-grade student who craves to be noticed and is uninhibited in achieving his or her goals sees you as a brand new attention-giver. This child will go beyond normal limits to divert attention away from your instruction and toward him or her. At first you choose to ignore the student's attempts to take over the class by shouting out answers prematurely. The student does not respond to your meaningful look or your controlled request, "Please raise your hand if you know the answer." Students are beginning to look at you as if to say, "Aren't you going to do something?" It may be time to:

- compliment him or her (please be specific) on a "job well done" today, and state that he or she has earned all the possible points and now it is important to hear from others;
- take away the student's audience by moving him or her to another part of the room, or even to another room if there is an agreement with another teacher; or
- request a conference with the student to commence as soon as the period is over, then discuss with him or her acceptable behavior in your class regarding class discussion.

The Reluctant Worker. All of your students with the exception of one have begun work on the twelfth-grade history assignment left by their teacher. You walk over to the student's desk and quietly ask that he or she begin work. What you receive is a blast far out of proportion to your request. "This is a stupid assignment, and I just don't want to do it!" You resist the urge to respond in kind and, in a controlled voice, state that:

- of course you can't make him or her do the work— however, if the student chooses not to do it, he or she will live with the consequences of a poor grade when his or her teacher returns and must explain the missing work and the behavior to the teacher tomorrow;
- you can see that the student feels the written work is an inappropriate assignment, but, because it is the only assignment we have right now, he or she might give it a try;
- you would like to talk about this issue at a later time, then pull out your plan book and determine a time to discuss it with the student; or
- the student can do the assignment work or go to time-out, a place where he or she can be quiet, not interact with other students, and consequently get himself or herself under control—it is the student's choice.

The Owl Squad. You are considering the removal of a student from your sixth-grade class because he or she has been highly confrontational and abusive with the other students in your science study group. It may be easier to discover what is causing the behavior than to attempt to control it. Acknowledge the student's feelings as you build rapport. After careful consideration, you could:

- give the student the choice of staying in the classroom and ceasing his or her belligerent acting out;
- send the student to the time-out room, though the student may state that he or she "will not go to time-out"—or "you can't make me!"—forcing you to try another tactic;
- give the student the choice of going to time-out on his own, or you will call in someone who will assist you in removing the student from the room; or
- avoid speaking to the student again but call in the "Owl Squad," or the "Who Squad," or the "School SWAT" team. (Whatever the name, most schools have a group of school personnel "on call" for such an emergency. They arrive quickly and ask one question: "Who?" The squad then escorts, physically, if necessary, the offender from the classroom. Fortunately, you had read about the Owl Squad in your sub packet and recognized this as a situation warranting such an action.) If no Owl Squad exists or there is no way to call the office, get help from a neighboring teacher.

Your Own Discipline Style

You will develop your own style of discipline. In any discipline situation, it is important that you act swiftly and with a calm, professional manner. As you work in different schools, pick up tips from teachers that you respect. They are on the job every day and generally are willing to share their successes and (a few of) their failures with colleagues.

Become a student of discipline, and keep a list of interventions that you believe are successful for you. Read a variety of sources. If one technique is less than adequate in a situation, try something else. The problems and the people change all the time, but you can improve your skills if you are willing to keep current and reflect on your handling of varied situations.

As a substitute, you are at a disadvantage because you must make professional decisions quickly and correctly with little background knowledge of the school or the students. It is your job to react quickly. One advantage that you have as a substitute is that you are in a position to compare many different classrooms and meet many teachers. This allows you to grow professionally in ways that perhaps regular teachers cannot. As a substitute teacher, you are learning that teaching children is an awesome and sometimes overwhelming task, but assisting children in the development of their self-discipline is perhaps an even greater challenge.

29

What Special Situations Might Occur?

Most substitute teachers become relatively comfortable with the normal routine after a few days' experience. When the assignment lasts for more than a day or two, it becomes necessary to prevent or take care of special situations that may arise. As a situation presents itself, remember to listen, think, and then react, if necessary. You may or may not have time or be able to ask students to help and, therefore, you may have to handle the situation on your own immediately. Find out what help may be available in emergencies. Never hesitate to ask questions so that you are prepared. After you have dealt with some of these special situations, you will feel more confident and able to "go with the flow" and handle any situation.

Switching Identities and Playing Hooky

One of students' favorite pranks is to switch seats and identities in the classroom. Because you usually do not know the students' names, and if you are without a seating chart, you might predict potential problems. Watch students come in and sit down. Is there a lot of grinning and/or giggling? If you suspect a prank developing, take the offensive. Try a getting-to-know-you activity, such as the ones described on page 17, or one of the brief starter activities suggested on pages 15–16. Get students involved immediately in a task that distracts them from their prank, and hopefully it will disappear. If you have a seating chart, look for vacant seats and start to make out an absentee form calling out the absent people. This will frequently stop the problem, especially when Richard must be absent because there is a girl sitting in his seat. Another more proactive idea is to get students busy on an assignment or ask for written homework (if any), and circulate, noting the names on their work. Then take attendance using your notes, and make your own seating chart. Remember it is not just your control of the class that is in jeopardy. You are responsible for an accurate recording of attendance, and good classroom management is the number one characteristic that principals require in first-year teachers and substitute teachers for continued employment.

If students report to you that one or more of their peers is playing hooky from your class because there is a substitute, it is very important that they are marked absent and you note this in your report to the regular classroom teacher. You should alert the office, but be sure the student really is absent. You should not be concerned that you may look foolish reporting someone absent who is not. You cannot afford to ignore the issue. Instead of looking foolish, you will appear to be "on the ball" and aware of who is in class. It also might work itself out if you keep making notes and observe closely what is going on in class. A neighboring teacher could provide insight into the situation or give suggestions related to a specific student.

Walking in Line

In the elementary school and in some middle schools, students are expected to line up and walk quietly and in an orderly fashion when moving from the classroom to the music room, auditorium, playground, or other destination outside of the classroom. Younger children are usually cooperative in doing this. They may be excited and bounce around some, but they usually get back in line when directed. Students in fourth through eighth grades may be more difficult for the substitute because they are more likely to use line movement to their advantage—to get a drink of water, to knock on doors, to make noise, to run instead of walk, to try to leave the line by running to a restroom, etc. Select a reliable student as line leader whom you have privately asked to lead the group to the desired location. Then most of your attention can be turned to the middle and end of the line where problems are more likely to take place. When working with younger children, you can frequently keep their hands busy and out of trouble by using a finger play, which requires using hand or finger movements while singing a song. With older students you may wish to take attendance again after you have reached your destination.

Emergency Procedures

Make sure that you are aware of the school's emergency procedures. Review the map of the school for the emergency exits, which are probably marked for emergency drills as are the "safe" locations during a fire, tornado, hurricane, and/or earthquake. If there is a drill or a real emergency situation, close or open doors and windows as directed by the emergency procedure. Always have your attendance list with you so that when the class has reached the designated location, you can immediately take roll again to verify that all your students reached the designated location. In some schools an older student runner reports each class's status to the principal. Once the drill is over and you have returned to the classroom, take roll one last time to make sure everyone is back. Report any student who you know is present at school, but is found missing at any point in an emergency procedure. Keeping students in line and together during these activities may be difficult, but, because you are responsible for the class, you do not want to lose any of them!

Pullout Programs

In many schools students will leave the regular classroom for "specials" and pullout programs during the day, especially in the case of elementary students. Pullout programs or "specials" require that the student leave the classroom to go to another room for specialized instruction, which includes band, choir, student government, speech, adaptive physical education, resource room for special education, etc. Hopefully, the regular classroom teacher has left information for you regarding such schedules. If not, one or two things may happen. First, the class may become distracted, putting their books away and watching the clock, signaling that it is time for the class to leave for a "special," such as physical education, which typically involves the entire class. Or an individual student may tell you that he or she is scheduled to go to speech or the resource room at a specific time. You must decide whether to trust the student. A reliable student in the class may be able to verify the schedule. Second, the "special" teacher may show up at the door to get the student or ask why he or she missed the session. You will have to use your best judgment in this area. In order to clarify which students are scheduled to go to which "special," you could:

- call the office or ask at the beginning of the day;
- ask an aide or "special" teacher;
- ask a neighboring teacher; or

- send a note to a "special" teacher for clarification.

If you decide to take the student's word, send a note with him or her to the "special" teacher with the student's name and time leaving the classroom. Tell the student that you want the "special" teacher to sign the note and return it to you when he or she returns.

Hall Passes

Hall passes are used in many schools when students must leave the classroom during a class session. Hand them out with caution, and periodically count them during the day so that they do not disappear. Students may need a pass to see the principal, nurse, or counselor, go to the library, or deliver something to another teacher. Judiciously used hall passes are very effective, but they may be abused by students when they all start asking to go to the restroom or to get a drink of water during class. Hopefully, a quick look at the classroom schedule will show you when time is allotted for these activities. Older students are expected to take care of these needs between classes. Be stern but fair. Some children have bladder problems (even in high school) or may feel ill and should be allowed an extra trip for these reasons.

Try a sign-out/sign-in system (including the time) as students are excused individually to leave the room briefly. Think ahead about the day's schedule, and plan periodic restroom breaks for students so that extra trips can be avoided.

Learn to make exceptions to the rules for the student who has a problem. If you do not, you may have to learn the hard way when you have to clean up the mess because there was no janitor available to help you. The accepted rule should be that if a student feels that he or she is about to make a mess, he or she has permission to go immediately to the restroom, and tell the teacher later.

Special Days

Some of the hardest days of the year to teach are days when there are parties, assemblies, or special programs. Substitutes frequently find these days even more difficult because the students start the day already "buzzed," and their levels of excitement grow until the

31

special event, usually at the end of the day. Try to keep the students busy at something interesting, fun, challenging, and motivating as much of the time as possible. Do not delve deeply into serious study material because students will lose interest due to the emotional nature of the day. You will have more control and a less frantic day.

You may also want to take some time before party time and assemblies to discuss appropriate behavior. Students will then know your expectations and may be less likely to misbehave.

Specific plans for such special activities may not be detailed within the regular teacher's plans. If there appear to be no supplies or plans for a party on a party day, you might check with the office. Generally, there are room parents in the elementary schools who help with class parties. Assemblies and special programs frequently require tickets or cards for attendance. Those students who are not attending may need to be escorted to a designated room. Because you are responsible for all of your students and their whereabouts during school hours, do not be reluctant to ask about these special situations.

Student Teachers

When you receive the call about an assignment, the caller may indicate that it will be a single day for you because the regular teacher is working with a student teacher. Depending on the stage of the student teacher's training, he or she may be responsible for teaching all, part, or none of the regular teacher's schedule. Because this information may not be explained in the regular teacher's plans, your first step is to interview the student teacher when you arrive to clarify the amount of responsibility the student teacher is accepting for the day. It is important to verify this with the principal.

If the student teacher is accepting responsibility for teaching all the lessons, it is your responsibility to observe but not intrude on the student teacher's authority, even if you disagree with the student teacher's decisions. Your role is to support the student teacher, as the regular teacher would do. You may choose to speak to the student teacher privately or

leave observation notes for the regular teacher, but the relationship that the student teacher is making with the students is more long-term than the one you will have with the class on a single day, and any conflicts expressed about the student teacher may undermine the relationship.

How Should You Serve Special Populations?

Whether you are substituting in kindergarten or twelfth grade, you must consider how you can ensure that the experience is as successful as possible for all students, including special needs students. Some of their needs are very similar to those of all students, while others present some serious challenges to teachers and school districts.

Mainstreaming and Inclusion

Since 1990, federal law mandates that schools provide for students with disabilities. P. L. 94–142, also called the Individuals with Disabilities Education Act (IDEA), requires that a school corporation must provide a free appropriate public education to students with disabilities in the least restrictive environment. Though some schools provide separate classrooms for special needs students or provide a resource room where these students go for special help in pullout programs, an increasing number of schools are using one of two approaches: mainstreaming or inclusion. Each of these programs manifests itself differently, and each will influence your day as a substitute. Therefore, it is imperative that you are familiar with how the school assists students with special needs.

Mainstreaming refers to the placement of special education students in regular education classes for part of the day. It is assumed that a mainstreamed student can participate with his or her peers by successfully completing most assignments required of other students in the class. The concept of mainstreaming has been the traditional approach toward ancillary services for special needs students. Typically, the goal for the mainstreamed student is to participate with his or her regular education peers in at least music, art, physical education, library, lunch, and recess. Thus, the mainstreamed student still receives academic instruction from the special education teacher.

Middle school and high school programs follow a similar format. Therefore, as you substitute, you may have students in your class who come and go in order to receive all of the special services they need and still participate in many programs with their class.

Inclusion is the other approach, in which the community makes a commitment to educate all children to the maximum extent possible in the school and classroom that they would normally attend whether they are special needs students or not. Inclusive programs include these students in the regular classroom and in all of its activities, unless they are physically incapable of doing so.

It is thought that a truly effective inclusion school is characterized by the virtual invisibility of the concept. Inclusion furthers the belief that students with disabilities will benefit from being in class with their nonhandicapped peers. These students should have the same opportunities as their peers. To create this environment, teachers adjust the delivery system to enable the student to function optimally in the regular classroom setting by bringing any individualized instruction to the special needs student. Special education personnel strive to work cooperatively with teachers in a team-teaching situation in the classroom by helping to meet the individual needs of both students with disabilities and those with none. With this collaborative effort in place, you may not be able to tell which students are disabled right away, unless someone tells you, and that is the whole idea.

When substituting, it is extremely important for you to remember that instructional aides or special education teachers are in the classroom regularly to assist you. It is imperative to know who these persons are and what roles they play in the education of the students. Often it will be your role to supervise the work of an aide and to work cooperatively with both the aide and the special education teacher. You must respect their judgments and contributions to the students' individual programs.

Working with Special Needs Students

If you are substituting for only one day, you may need to do little to accommodate special needs students. However, if you remain with that class for longer than a day, you may be expected to adapt curriculum and instruction involving homework assignments, tests, quizzes, grades, the environment, and assistive devices. Seek assistance when it becomes apparent this will be your responsibility.

You must consider adaptations of classroom instruction in each specific content area. Though there are a limited number of suggestions that can be provided here, refer to the bibliography in Chapter 9 for further insight. In modifying instructions for writing assignments, you may plan to:

- reduce the length and/or complexity;
- allow more time for completion;
- avoid penalizing students for spelling, punctuation, or grammar errors;
- allow students to dictate their answers to peers, parents, or an aide; or
- allow students to use a tape recorder or other device.

For reading assignments, you may need to:

- tape stories and chapters;
- allow students to work with a peer; or
- recognize the value of listening comprehension and permit the student to participate in only parts of the activity.

When looking at homework assignments, you may be expected to:

- communicate expectations to parents;
- reduce the assignments;
- provide clear and concise directions with time lines recorded in a homework log; or
- allow homework papers to be typed by the student or dictated and then recorded by someone else.

Tests, quizzes, or grades may be adjusted for the student who needs:

- the test read orally;
- the number of items on the test reduced;

33

- terminology or concepts simplified;
- the test readministered at a later date; or
- his or her grade modified, with the evaluation based on individual student improvement or the use of a pass/fail system.

Environmental adaptations may include matching seating arrangements with students' particular physical needs or allowing students to take short breaks from classroom activities. Many students may need such assistive devices as communication books, boards, cards, computer devices, or environmental control devices.

It is important for you to work effectively with all students. The more you know and understand about working with special needs students the more effective you will be and the less disruptive they will be in your class. Enjoy the experience as an opportunity for your own growth as well as to help the students in your charge to do the same.

34

Chapter 5

Elementary School Lesson Activities

What Is an Elementary School?

Tables full of science projects, multicolored butterflies cascading down the halls, cartoon characters reminding students to use their best manners or wash their hands before eating. Movement. Lines of walking, sliding, bouncing children. These images evoke the joyful learning contained in elementary schools today. Traditionally divided into primary (K–2) and intermediate (3–5) levels, each grade level has one or more teachers depending on the number of students. In addition to the traditional structure, an elementary school may be configured in many ways, from multilevel rooms to ungraded classes.

Of course, many schools still reflect the picture of a single teacher with 15–30 children grouped by grade level. However, within this familiar structure are many deviations. Children are pulled out for special needs such as speech therapy or English instruction, or because they are learning disabled or gifted. Whole classes may attend "specials" like art, music, physical education, computer instruction, library, or media classes. Children whose special needs were once served in resource or special education classes are now mainstreamed or included in regular classrooms, with aides or inclusion teachers working alongside the classroom teachers. Teachers may retain the sole responsibility for teaching or share it in team-teaching situations.

Elementary curriculum still centers on the exciting tasks of readin', 'ritin', and 'rithmatic. But the methods that teachers and administrators use to achieve learning vary widely. Some elementary schools center their reading programs on the Whole Language approach, where children learn to read through their own writing and by critically listening to stories. Other schools maintain a phonetic approach. Still others blend several reading methods. Mathematics may be taught as a problem-solving process with less emphasis on right answers than on methods of solving problems. Science may consist of hands-on experiments, and social studies may be taught or augmented through literature and art.

Whole schools now choose to embrace specific theories such as Gardner's (1983) Multiple Intelligences or Adler's (1982) Paedeia system of instruction. These and other curricular trends may be found across the country in abundance. Thus, each elementary school becomes its own culture, which an effective substitute must learn to navigate.

What Are Elementary Students Like?

Elementary school students are in the heart of their childhood. During the five or six years they attend elementary school, children progress from a preoperational learning stage to preadolescent, from self- and family-centered to peer-influenced. The years from 5 to 11 are critical to students' development. They enter elementary school learning letters and numbers. They leave being able to write stories and perform mathematical operations.

Primary students—grades K–2—are a very active bunch. In kindergarten, they learn how to be students, both socially and academically. They learn how to cope with other children vying for the teacher's attention, how to sit in desks, how to walk in lines, how to recognize letters and numbers and what those symbols mean. First grade provides "real" readers, and second graders delve more deeply into all subjects while still wanting to "please the teacher." Younger children have short attention spans and limited sitting abilities. Having been exposed to countless 15- and 30- second television commercials, children are conditioned to expect information in short bursts. Consequently, teachers must now help them respond to longer, more complicated pieces of information. As concrete learners, students of this age require much hands-on activity. At the very least, they must be able to imagine concrete references in order to understand. Their

learning, art, music, and play are full of stories. Listening to the monologue of a concentrating K–2 child is hearing his or her thought processes aloud.

Intermediate-aged children in grades 3–5 read better, are capable of more independent projects, and are more socially centered. By third grade, socialization is gender based. Groups of boys and groups of girls reflect the social nature of the children. They are able to accomplish more complicated tasks in groups, assigning and assuming roles necessary to make group work successful. Fourth grade finds some girls beginning early puberty. At this level, the girls begin to mature more quickly than the boys, who make up for it a few years later. Fourth and fifth grades are a very social time. Peer pressure is prominent as preadolescence emerges. Consequently, teacher approval may seem less important than peer approval. Recognizing their own and others' academic strengths and weaknesses, students are also capable of maintaining interest in a topic over a longer period of time.

What Responsibilities Might You Have?

The first responsibility of an elementary substitute teacher is to find out as much as possible about the school and the students. Ask the principal, the school secretary, and other teachers about academic and behavioral expectations. Is this a school where all disciplinary actions are kept in the classroom? Or does the principal wish to have his or her hand in responding to most problems? Is there a school-wide management plan, or does each teacher provide his or her own rules and consequences? Where can you find your teacher's management plan? Which of the students might be most helpful in locating items or indicating how things are done? It is also helpful to know little things like how students line up—single file or in gender-specific double lines.

When you arrive in the classroom, check first for lesson plans. You will find variation between teachers' plans. Some teachers provide direction rather than specific planning. Others will over-plan, believing it is better to have too much planned than too little. As you read through the plans, locate the materials necessary to complete the plans, and place them in the order that you will need them. Note any irregularities in the schedule (special classes, students, school events), and circle them. Note where you may fit in special lessons you have prepared. Then scan the room for name tags. If you do not see any, find some materials for the students to make them.

As a substitute, you will be responsible for attendance, lunch count (don't forget yourself!), milk money, and other clerical tasks accomplished at the beginning of a school day. Helpful students will let you know the "right" way to do these things. You may also be asked to watch children during recess, lunch, or while they get on and off busses. Once again, finding out what the behavioral expectations are will make the job go more smoothly. Additional duties should be noted in your lesson plans.

One issue concerning your responsibilities is that of correcting work. If you understand what the teacher expects from assignments, by all means correct the papers. Leave them in a place where the teacher may look them over before returning to students. Finally, write the teacher a note indicating your successes and difficulties. Don't go on about what a bad kid Angela was that day. Simply indicate that she had difficulty participating fairly in the spelling bee. You may also indicate that you appreciated the opportunity to work with his or her students and look forward to doing so again.

One other facet that may ensure your success as a substitute is your "bag of tricks." Carry it with you to each school. In it you will find the lessons in this chapter, which are sure-fire-success lessons. You will also find management techniques that work really well

for you, as well as games, books, videos, or other "treats" to offer productive, well-behaved classes at the end of the day.

In the following part of this chapter, you will find lesson plans developed by veteran teachers. Take advantage of their expertise. Create your own plans or modify the existing ones. In addition, here are some other tips that will help you find success as an elementary substitute teacher.

1. Employ teaching strategies that involve more than listening or looking from the students. Small children like to move, touch, dance, and sing while they learn. But keep a lid on it by having a few children demonstrate at a time.

2. Prepare name tags and use students' names every chance you get. It personalizes your interactions with the students, regardless of age.

3. Move. Do not sit in one place. Be near as many students as possible as you conduct discussions, get ready to leave the room, or go from one activity to another.

4. Give students something to do or think about when they are in line. For example, sing a song (softly if you must), do a finger-play, make up a marching cadence, or have students count something as they walk.

5. The best way to eliminate management problems is to keep students busy all of the time. Extra activities are really helpful to keep in your "bag of tricks."

6. Listen to the students. You will learn a great deal about the world from their unique point of view. In all probability you will have at least one chuckle as you learn.

37

Choosing the Main Idea

Gloria J. Shelton • Grade 2 Teacher • Lawton, OK

Student Objectives

The students will be able to:
- explain what a paragraph is.
- identify the main idea of a paragraph.

Materials Needed

Students:
- reading textbook
- "Choosing the Main Idea" worksheet
- pencil

New Terminology

paragraph: a group of sentences that deals with a particular point or idea

main idea: the most important point of the paragraph; what the paragraph stresses

Lesson Activity Process

Clock 25–35 minutes.

The teacher will:
1. Ask students to get out their reading books and together choose one of the students' favorite stories.
2. Read the story out loud to the class.
3. Tell students that most stories are written in paragraphs—groups of sentences that deal with a particular, or main, idea.
4. Read the story's first paragraph again. Ask students to identify the main idea of the paragraph.
5. Repeat the exercise with the second paragraph.
6. When it is clear from their answers that the students understand the concept of *main idea*, distribute copies of the worksheet titled, "Choosing the Main Idea."
7. Now continue to read the story aloud, paragraph by paragraph. Ask students to write down, by each paragraph number, one or two words to describe the main idea in that paragraph. You can do the first two together as a class.

Modifications for Students with Special Needs

- Print student answers for each paragraph on the chalkboard, and allow students to copy the words onto their worksheets.

- Have students use a glue stick to trace the vocabulary words (tactile involvement), then ask students to trace the gluey words with their fingers. Provide students with wipes for cleanup.

Evaluation

Use the completed worksheets for evaluation purposes.

Answers to Student Worksheet

Answers will vary, depending on the story used.

Tips for Success

- Make sure that the directions for the worksheet are explained completely and that each student understands what to do.
- Be sure adequate time is provided for all students to write their answers on the worksheet before you proceed to the next paragraph.
- As you wait for students to write each answer, create your own list of paragraph numbers and their corresponding main ideas for use in evaluating completed worksheets.
- If you are unable to photocopy the worksheet, its contents can be copied onto the chalkboard or printed on a transparency for an overhead projector. In this case, the class as a whole would identify each paragraph's main idea, and volunteers could print the answers on the board or transparency.

Additional Related Activities

1. Have students draw a picture illustrating one of the main ideas from the paragraphs just read. Under the drawing, students could write the main idea their pictures represent.
2. Try this exercise with a book students have not yet read. The school or classroom library will have a grade-appropriate book.

Notes for Next Time

Reading Student Page

Choosing the Main Idea

Name ______________________ Date __________ Class __________

Write down the main idea of each paragraph.

Paragraph 1 ____

____

Paragraph 2 ____

____

Paragraph 3 ____

____

Paragraph 4 ____

____

Paragraph 5 ____

____

Paragraph 6 ____

____

Paragraph 7 ____

____

Paragraph 8 ____

____

Paragraph 9 ____

____

Paragraph 10 ____

____

Debra I. Gowins • Kindergarten Teacher • Bowling Green, KY

Pick, Choose, and Group Categorization

Language Arts

Student Objectives

The students will be able to:
- be more aware of their surroundings.
- recognize likenesses and differences in objects by categorizing them into groups.

Materials Needed

Teacher:
- chalkboard, posterboard, chart paper, or erasable easel board
- appropriate writing utensil

Students:
- pencil
- crayons
- paper

New Terminology

group: two or more people or things that are together
categorize: grouping things that are alike
classify: to put in a category or group
New vocabulary words may also be introduced while listing the objects during the activity.

Lesson Activity Process

Clock 15–20 minutes.
The teacher will:

1. Ask all students with brown eyes to stand on the left side of the room and all students with blue eyes to stand on the right. Ask all students with eyes not brown or blue to stand in the front of the room. Explain that you just used students' eye color to classify them; that is, you created groups of children according to eye color.
2. Now draw a line on the chalkboard. (Guess at the placement of the line by observing the average height of the students.) Tell students to file up to the board, row by row. Each student should stand at the line you have drawn. If the student is taller than the height of the line, the student should stand on the left side of the class. If the student is shorter, ask him or her to stand on the right. When all the students have measured themselves ask, What did I use to categorize you into groups this time? (Height)

3. After students have returned to their seats, explain that you are going to play a grouping game. Show them how to start the game by retrieving any object in the classroom as the students silently count to 20 (or students can watch the clock for 20 seconds). At the end of the 20-count, students should raise their hands, indicating it is time for you to go back to your seat with your chosen object.
4. Repeat this procedure for each row of students, until all the students have an object to share with the class.
5. Students should then name their objects as you list them on the chalkboard.
6. Now ask students to choose items from the list that have things in common. Have those items brought to a common tabletop.
7. Discuss why all the items on the table fit into a certain category or group. Have students think of one name to call all the items that have something in common.
8. Repeat this grouping activity until most of the objects students chose belong to one category or another.

Modifications for Students with Special Needs

- Start with general categories. Categorize things by color, size, etc., before going to more specific categories—things with wheels, things you can read, etc.
- Have pairs of students, rather than individual students, search for an object in the class.

Evaluation

Ask students to draw pictures of three items that could be grouped together. Underneath their pictures, ask students to print a word that identifies what the three items have in common—nonwriters will need your help with this.

Tips for Success

- If, as students group themselves, you find they are having difficulty with their behavior, you may wish to limit the number of students who will retrieve objects for the grouping game. In larger classes, you may wish to limit the number to 10 or 15 students.
- During the open discussion-and-answer segment of this activity, do not force any child to respond. Many children learn by listening and are not comfortable in

a large group setting or with an unfamiliar face in the classroom.

- Encourage the students to help spell words as they are listed on the board.
- Consider the age and development of the students when determining how much guidance to offer in grouping items.
- Use familiar words such as *same, different, alike,* and *not alike.*

Additional Related Activities

1. After categorizing the students by eye color and height, ask students if they can think of any other ways in which they could be grouped. (Students may suggest categorizing by eye color and height together, by clothing or hair color, by gender, by shoe styles, etc.)

2. Each student can draw a picture on a Post-it note of the item he or she chose. Then have students use the Post-it pictures to create a categorization graph on the chalkboard.

3. Lead a discussion in which students try to categorize something they can't see in the classroom—kinds of foods, vehicles, television shows, etc.

Notes for Next Time

Writing about Dinosaurs

Amy Somerville • Grade 1 Teacher • Springfield, TN

Composition

Student Objectives

The students will be able to:

- practice comprehension skills.
- improve listening skills.
- think and write creatively.

Materials Needed

Teacher:

- book about dinosaurs—the school library should have several grade-appropriate books.

Students:

- paper
- pencil

New Terminology

None

Lesson Activity Process

Clock 15–20 minutes.
The teacher will:

1. Show the book to the class and ask the students what they think the story will be about.
2. Lead a discussion in which students tell what they have already learned about dinosaurs.
3. Now explain that you will read the book aloud to the class. Tell students to listen carefully, because when you are finished reading, each student will be asked to retell the story to a partner.
4. Read the book and show students the pictures.
5. Pair up the students, and have the pairs retell the story to each other.
6. Now tell students they are going to write a new story about dinosaurs. Write on the chalkboard, "Dizzy Dinosaur's First Day." Tell students to imagine that a dinosaur named Dizzy has come back to walk the earth. Ask students to offer sentences that together will tell the story of Dizzy Dinosaur's first day back. Print on the chalkboard the sentences students offer.

Modifications for Students with Special Needs

- Have a peer helper draw a picture whose details are dictated by the special needs student.
- Have a group of students put the pictures created for the class's evaluation in order for the class book.

Evaluation

Ask each student to draw a picture illustrating one page of information from the dinosaur book. Then put the pages in order and staple them together to create the class's own dinosaur book. Primary criteria should be the students' accuracy of the story line and the descriptive observations they make as they retell the story.

Tips for Success

- Several books lend themselves to this activity. One is Most's *If the Dinosaurs Came Back.* Others include Carrick's *What Happened to Patrick's Dinosaurs?* and *Big Bad Bones*; Brenner's *Dinosaurium*; Aliki's *My Visit to the Dinosaurs*; and Dixon's *The Illustrated Dinosaur Encyclopedia.*
- If possible, familiarize yourself with the book you have chosen ahead of time.
- Remember to share the book's illustrations with the students.
- The story created by students should stay short—five or six sentences would probably be long enough.
- Place other appropriate dinosaur books in the room for students whose interest has been stimulated by the discussion.

42

Additional Related Activities

1. Talk about how big dinosaurs were. Tell students that the meat-eating Tyrannosaurus Rex was 40 feet long! If an encyclopedia is available, show students a picture of a Tyrannosaurus Rex. Then take students out into the hall, and place a bit of tape on the floor as a starting point. Use a yardstick, and have students count 13 yardstick lengths with you. Add one foot and put a bit of tape at your 40-foot mark. Now have students lie in a row, head to toe, from tape to tape, to see how many "children-long" a Tyrannosaurus Rex was.

2. Students who are already reading can read other books about dinosaurs and tell these new stories to the class.

3. Talk about whether students would like to have a pet dinosaur. Could it live in their homes? What would it eat?

4. Have a student copy the story from the chalkboard. Ask a student to read the story aloud.

Notes for Next Time

Counting Coins

Mathematics

Merri Lynne Hinton • Library Media Specialist • Guthrie, KY

Student Objectives

The students will be able to:
- count money by combining various coins.
- classify coins.

Materials needed

Teacher:
- overhead projector
- real coins: one half-dollar, three quarters, five dimes, five nickels, and five pennies

Students:
- coins handout
- "Counting Coins" worksheet
- scissors
- paper
- pencil

New Terminology

None

Lesson Activity Process

Clock 25–30 minutes.

The teacher will:

1. Distribute to each student a copy of the coins handout, and direct students to cut out the coins.
2. Place your real coins in a pile on the overhead projector. Now tell students you need 50 cents for the juice machine. Ask, "What coins should I use?"
3. When a student answers correctly, ask that student to illustrate his or her answer with the real coins on the overhead projector, while students recreate each coin combination with their paper coins.
4. Then ask students to use their paper coins to come up with different coin combinations that add up to 50 cents. Have volunteers illustrate each correct answer with the real coins on the overhead projector. Also ask a student to write the combinations on the chalkboard. Students should identify some of the following combinations: one half-dollar; two quarters; one quarter plus two dimes plus one nickel; five dimes; four dimes plus two nickels; three dimes plus four nickels.

5. For extra credit, ask students to imagine their pockets are full of other coins. What other coin combinations add up to 50 cents? Students may identify the following: 10 nickels; 6 nickels plus 2 dimes; 50 pennies, etc.
6. Now distribute copies of the "Counting Coins" worksheet for students to complete independently.

Modifications for Students with Special Needs

- Have peer helpers hold two papers together and cut two sets of coins simultaneously, one for the helper and one for the special needs student.
- Have students work in pairs, with one set of paper coins, to determine coin combinations.

Evaluation

As one student recreates his or her coin combination on the overhead projector, check the paper coin selections of several students. Repeat this with a new group of students each time a new coin combination is identified and illustrated. In addition, the completed worksheets can be used for evaluation purposes.

Answers to Student Worksheet

The following combinations all add up to 32 cents: one quarter plus one nickel plus two pennies; one dime plus four nickels plus two pennies; three dimes plus two pennies.

Tips for Success

- Give students enough time to cut out all their coins. Ask those who finish early to help others.
- If available, David M. Schwartz's *If You Made a Million*, which shows different ways of making an amount of money, can help set the stage for this money-counting activity.
- To make working in front of the class at the overhead projector a positive experience, ask each student to tell you the combination of coins before he or she goes to the overhead projector. If the student's answer is not correct, go to the student's desk and use the paper coins to help figure out the mistake. Then the student will be able to determine the correct answer before illustrating it on the overhead projector.

44

Additional Related Activities

1. Divide the class into small groups and ask each group to pick some amount (no larger than a dollar). Then have group members use all their coins together to determine how many combinations of coins can be used to equal the chosen amount. Which group came up with the most combinations?

2. To provide an opportunity for students to practice counting money in a realistic situation, set up a "post office" using stickers as stamps. Students must count out their paper coins to buy the "stamps," and the postal worker must give the appropriate change.

3. Tell students they are going to play the Penny Trading Game. Divide the class into small groups, and choose a volunteer in each group to act as the group's banker. Each student in the group will, in turn, roll a die and get that number of pennies from the banker. Each time the student gets enough money, he or she trades for a coin of equal value. For example, when the student has five pennies, he or she will trade for one nickel. The game can continue until someone in the group reaches a dollar or as long as you would like.

Notes for Next Time

Counting Coins

Name _____ **Date** _____ **Class** _____

A stamp to mail a letter costs 32 cents. Use your paper coins to combine enough coins to buy one stamp. You can make three coin combinations that equal 32 cents. Write below how many of each coin you will combine to equal 32 cents.

	Combination 1 How many?	Combination 2 How many?	Combination 3 How many?
half-dollar			
quarter			
dime			
nickel			
penny			

46

Extra Credit:
If you only had a half-dollar, how much change would you get when you bought one stamp?

50¢ 25¢ 25¢ 25¢ 1¢ 1¢

10¢ 10¢ 10¢ 10¢ 10¢ 1¢

5¢ 5¢ 5¢ 5¢ 5¢ 1¢ 1¢

Building a Better Airplane

Steven W. Sanders • Grades 4–5 Science Teacher • Bowling Green, KY

Student Objectives

Students will be able to:

- follow directions in constructing a paper airplane.
- understand that the design of an airplane affects its flight.
- build measuring skills.
- formulate averages.

Materials Needed

The teacher may wish to use one of the many books available to obtain additional blueprints for paper airplanes as supplements to the worksheet.

Students:

- "Building a Better Airplane" worksheet
- patterns for the Victoria and the Addie planes
- paper (this can be recycled paper)
- pencil

New Terminology

None

Lesson Activity Process

Clock 35–45 minutes.
The teacher will:

1. Divide students into groups of three or four, and distribute copies of the two paper airplane patterns to each group.
2. Tell the groups that each student in the group should use a blank sheet of paper to construct one of the paper airplanes. Students also may wish to create their own design.
3. When all the students have finished their planes, have the first group approach a "flight area" that you have predesignated. Between the desk rows might be appropriate. Then you could have more than one group fly its planes at the same time. One at a time, each group member should step up to the starting line and launch his or her plane.
4. Have the group measure the stride of one of its members. Then the group should count the number of strides it takes for the member to reach each plane after each flight. The number of strides times the

number of inches in the stride will give the distance traveled by the plane. This distance should be recorded by every member of the group on his or her "Building a Better Airplane" worksheet.

5. Each student's plane should make three flights. After all planes in a group have made their flights and their flight distances have been recorded, the students will leave the flight area and begin to average the three distances for each plane. Members should record these averages on the worksheet.
6. Repeat steps 3–5 for each group in the class until all planes have made three flights.
7. Have each group discuss the average distances of all the planes in the group and decide upon the best plane design.
8. Ask a spokesperson from each group to tell the class which design the group chose and how it made this decision.

Modifications for Students with Special Needs

- Use peer helpers to help construct planes for those who lack the manual dexterity required.
- Have a set of prefolded planes available.

Evaluation

Observe the participation of each member of the group. Did each member complete his or her model? Did each member attempt to fly his or her plane? Did each member collect his or her data on the worksheet? All of these factors should be included when evaluating the student's performance. The distance traveled by the plane should have no effect on the student's grade in this particular activity.

Answers to Student Worksheet

Answers will vary according to the data collected. Students should have all data recorded in the "Group Data" section of the worksheet. Students should have the correct average recorded for each airplane in their group. The "Class Data" section is optional.

47

Tips for Success

- Circulate throughout the class to ensure that all students are averaging their data properly and that these averages are being recorded.
- If possible, make arrangements to use the gym or another large room for the test flights.
- If you wish, place masking tape on the floor, with meters marked off, in place of having the students walk the flight distances.
- Prior to the test flights, ask students to predict which plane will fly the farthest and to explain their choices.
- When grouping the children, avoid the "boys against the girls" contest. This activity should encourage the development of cooperative working skills with all students.
- If the weather permits, the flights can be made outside.

48

Notes for Next Time

Additional Related Activities

1. See if the school library has any books available on paper airplane design. Some you can look for are *The Paper Airplane*, by Seymour Simon; *Paper Airplanes*, by Nick Robinson; and *Fabulous Paper Airplanes*, by E. Richard Churchill. Then allow students to choose among many designs for their plane construction. In addition, students whose interest is piqued by this activity can learn more about paper airplanes from these books.

2. After each group averages the distances of its planes, the group should choose its best design. The best design from each group will compete in the class finals. The data from this competition should be recorded in the "Class Data" section of the worksheet.

3. Tell students that their job is to design airplanes for a large company. They are asked to design a new plane. This plane can be any design that they wish as long as it meets the design specifications.
   - The plane must carry at least 50 persons.
   - The plane must be able to travel long distances.
   - The plane must have *at least* 3 engines.

The designer must draw a picture of his or her plane and include labels to show that the plane meets the design specifications.

Building a Better Airplane

Name _____ Date _____ Class _____

Group Data

Name	Trial 1	Trial 2	Trial 3	Average

49

Class Data

Name	Trial 1	Trial 2	Trial 3	Average

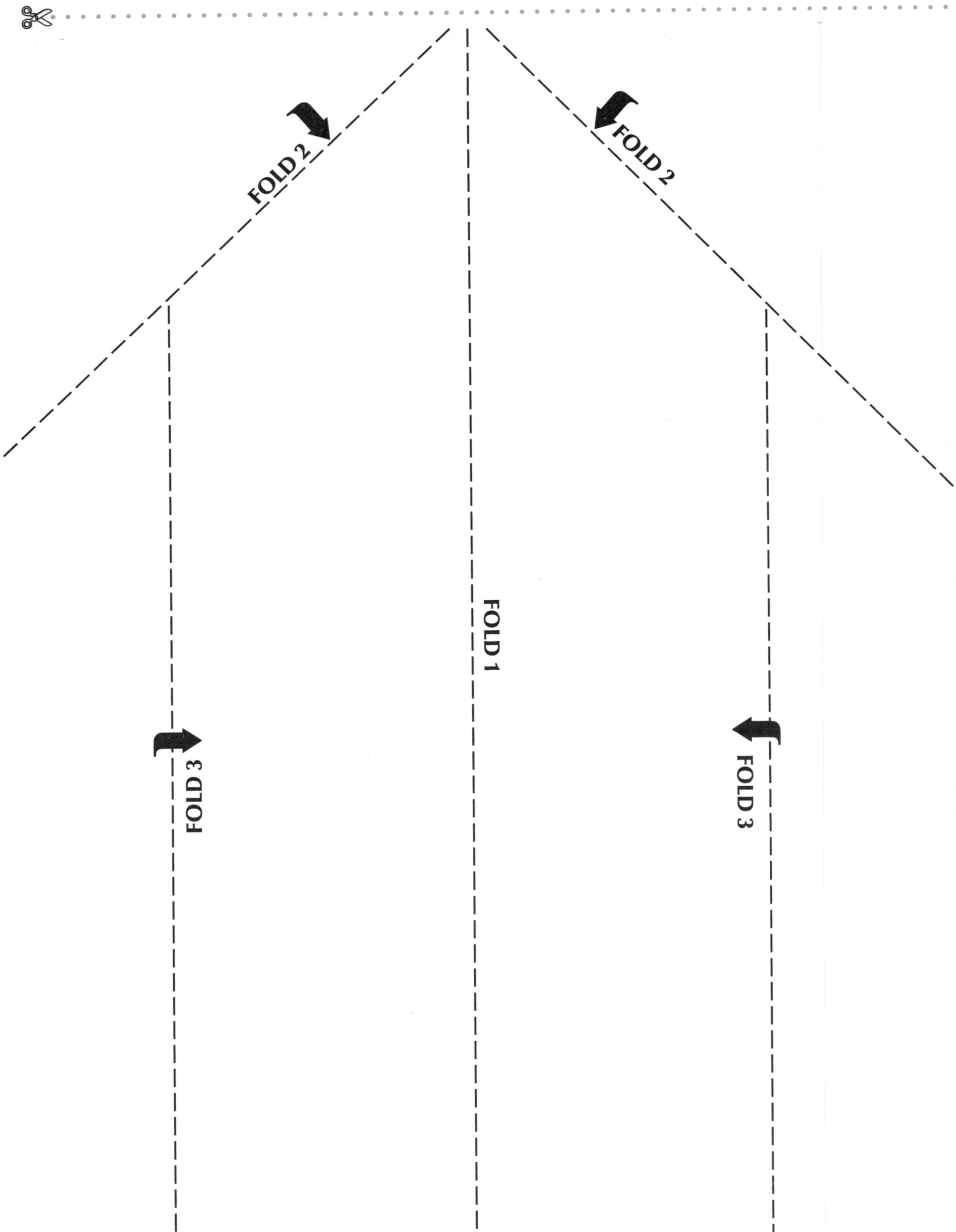

FOLD 2

FOLD 2

FOLD 1

FOLD 3

FOLD 3

The Victoria Single Engine

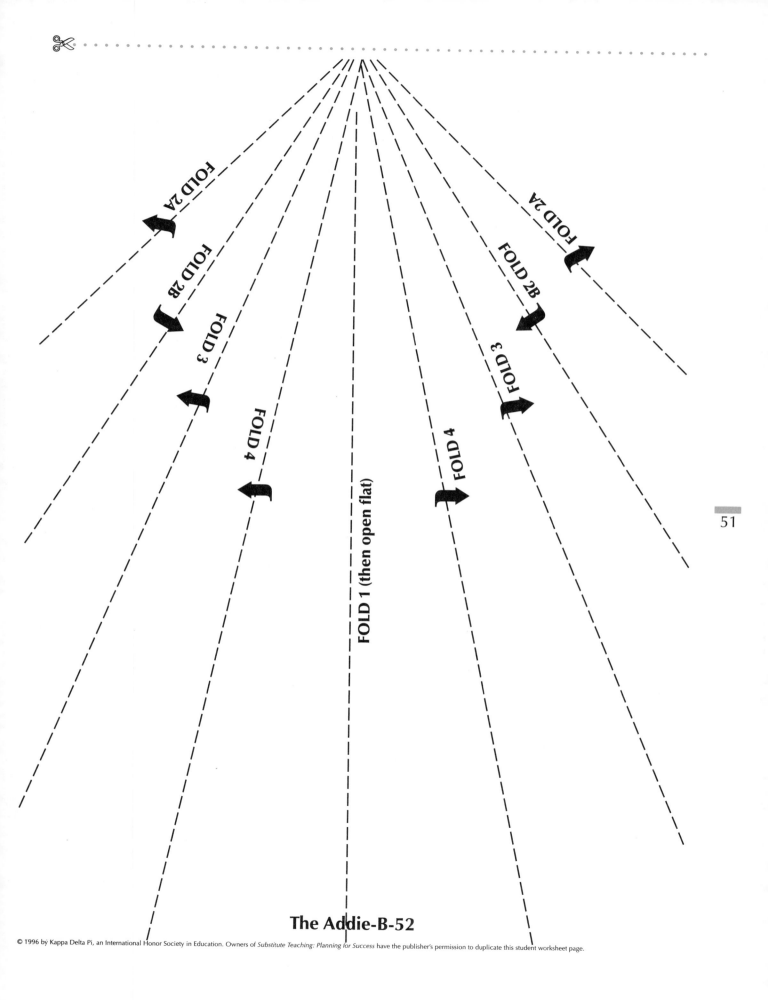

FOLD 2A

FOLD 2A

FOLD 2B

FOLD 2B

FOLD 3

FOLD 3

FOLD 4

FOLD 4

FOLD 1 (then open flat)

51

The Addie-B-52

Learning Lines of Latitude

Richard A. Rutherford • Grade 5 Teacher • Vincennes, IN

Student Objectives

Students will be able to:

- recognize lines of latitude on a globe.
- identify the location of specific latitude lines.

Materials Needed

- globe

New Terminology

lines of latitude: imaginary lines that extend around the Earth from east to west

Equator: an imaginary line of latitude that circles the Earth exactly halfway between the North and South poles

axis: imaginary rod through the center of the Earth on which the Earth spins

North Pole: the northernmost end of the Earth's axis

South Pole: the southernmost end of the Earth's axis

Tropic of Cancer: latitude line north of the Equator

Tropic of Capricorn: latitude line south of the Equator

Arctic Circle: latitude line between the North Pole and the Tropic of Cancer

Antarctic Circle: latitude line between the South Pole and the Tropic of Capricorn

Lesson Activity Process

Clock 35–45 minutes.

The teacher will:

1. Draw a circle on the chalkboard and explain that the circle represents the Earth.

2. Show a globe to the class. Explain that lines of latitude are imaginary lines that, along with longitude lines, help people find their way around the Earth.

3. Tell students that some lines of latitude have names. The Equator is one example. Ask if any student knows where the Equator is. Have a volunteer come to the globe and point to the Equator. As students are identifying latitude lines on the globe, have a volunteer draw in and label the lines on the circle.
   In the same way, ask volunteers to use the globe to identify the North and South poles; the Arctic and Antarctic circles; and the Tropics of Cancer and Capricorn. If students are unfamiliar with the location of any of these latitude lines, have volunteers search the globe to identify them.

4. Tell the students to imagine their bodies are globes. Direct students to stand with their feet together. Now use the chalkboard drawing to review the Equator's position and ask where the Equator would be found on their bodies (around their waists). Review the positions of the North and South poles, and ask where the poles would be found (top of head; bottom of feet). Review the locations of the Arctic and Antarctic circles, and ask students to identify where these latitude lines would be (around the temple area; around the ankles). Review the positions of the Tropics of Cancer and Capricorn, and ask students to find each tropic on the body (shoulders and knees).

Modifications for Students with Special Needs

- Have physically challenged students answer verbally rather than pointing to identify latitude lines.
- Use a drawing of a person and ask students with special needs to point to the imagined location of each specific latitude line.

Evaluation

Play a game. Call out each latitude line that was discussed to see if the children can point to the location of each on their bodies. Begin slowly, then build up to calling them out quickly.

Tips for Success

- You may wish to begin this lesson by holding up the globe and asking students to relate what they already know about the Earth.
- Remind students that the Earth is not situated exactly up and down. Instead, it tilts on its axis.

52

Additional Related Activities

1. Divide the class into small groups, and give each group a balloon and a marker. Tell the groups they are to imagine the balloon is a globe. Their assignment is to use the marker to draw on their balloon "Earth" the lines discussed in class. Students can use the drawing on the board for reference.

2. Display a climate map of the world. Then lead a discussion in which students determine whether different places along the same line of latitude experience similar climates.

3. Have a volunteer stand still to represent the sun. Then ask a volunteer to take the globe on an orbit around the sun. Remind the volunteer that, as the Earth orbits around the sun, it also spins on its axis. Ask students to watch the demonstration. Then ask which motion brings us day and night—rotation around Earth's axis. Then ask which motion brings us our 365-day year—revolution around the sun.

Notes for Next Time

53

Playing Beach Ball Volleyball

Kathy Bristow • Middle School Physical Education Teacher • Libertyville, IL

Student Objectives

The students will be able to:

- work cooperatively in a volleyball-type game.
- show a basic understanding of the rules of volleyball.
- understand the basics of scoring in volleyball.
- have fun while playing fairly.

Materials Needed

Teacher:

- one large beach ball
- net (set 3–4 feet high for grades K–3; 5 feet high for grades 4 and 5)

Students:

- "Playing Beach Ball Volleyball" worksheet
- pencil

New Terminology

serve: start the ball

set: a hit with both hands when the ball is shoulder-high or higher

forearm pass or **bump:** a hit, below shoulder level, in which both hands are clasped and the ball is hit with the forearms by shrugging the shoulders

double hit: when one person hits the ball two (or more) times in a row, with no one else touching the ball between hits

Lesson Activity Process

Clock 20–25 minutes.

The teacher will:

1. Begin the lesson by explaining to students that the only way to get good at something is to practice. That's true in anything—learning your multiplication tables, riding your bike, or playing ball. But it's hard to practice, or even to try, if you're afraid someone is going to make fun of you. So, in this game, if any student makes fun of someone else, the offending student will have to lose his or her turn and go to the end of the line.

2. Tell students that they are going to play beach ball volleyball. Have students count off by twos; then take the first six "1's" to make up the first team, and the first six "2's" to make up the second team.

3. Explain that, in this game, the object is to get the ball over the net from one side to the other, again and again, until one team misses. But, as with any game, there are rules to follow:
   - Only two-handed hits will count.
   - Any number of hits per side is okay, but no person can hit it two times in a row.
   - Students cannot touch the net.
   - Students should "call the ball" (they can say "Mine" or "I've got it").
   - a point is scored only when your team serves.

4. Allow the two teams to play the game until one side wins with a score of five points. Then retire those two teams and send the next 12 students onto the court.

5. For upper grades, after all the students have had a chance to play, pass out copies of the worksheet for students to complete. For lower grades, read the worksheet and allow students to offer verbal responses.

NOTE: The last three terms—receiving team, legal hit, and sideout—were not mentioned as vocabulary terms. See if students can figure these three out from their experiences playing the game.

Modifications for Students with Special Needs

- Have all students sit in chairs to complete this activity.
- Adjust the net's height to promote successful hits.
- Use a Nerf ball.

Evaluation

You will have the opportunity to observe the students in groups of 12 as two teams play each other. Watch to see whether students indicate a basic understanding of the rules as the game progresses. This, rather than a student's proficiency with the ball, should serve as the basis for evaluation.

Written or verbal responses to the worksheet can be used for evaluation purposes.

54

Answers to Student Worksheet

1–4. see terminology above.

5. receiving team—the team that cannot make points.

6. legal hit—a hit using two hands (a set or a forearm pass).

7. sideout—when the serving team loses its serve.

Tips for Success

- never leave students unsupervised.
- remind students that in physical education, safety always comes first.
- be aware of students with any special medical needs—like asthma, diabetes, students who suffer from seizures, and those allergic to bee stings—as described by the teacher, or ask students.
- report any accidents or injuries to the nurse or office, and file a report when necessary.
- encourage and recognize fair play and sportsmanlike behavior.
- ask students on the sidelines to cheer for both teams.
- after all the students have had a chance to play, mix up the class to form new teams and start again, as time permits.
- feel free to modify the rules and equipment—number of students on a team, number of points needed to win, height of the net—whenever modifications will encourage student success.

Notes for Next Time

Additional Related Activities

1. Have students play a game of Balloon-Keep-It-Up. Divide students into teams of 4–6 players each. Give each team a large round balloon. Tell the teams that the object of the game is to keep the balloon up in the air as long as they can, using only two-handed hits—sets and forearm passes. As in the beach ball volleyball game, no double hits are allowed. If you wish, you can use punchballs instead of balloons—this equipment change will speed up the game.

2. Have students form a line, with several feet between students. Toss a balloon to the last person in the line. Then have each student use only sets and forearm passes to pass the balloon forward to the next student, until the balloon reaches the first person in the line.

3. If students appear proficient at beach ball volleyball, play the game with an additional rule: The ball cannot be hit more than three times on a side before it must go over the net.

55

Playing Beach Ball Volleyball

Name _____ **Date** _____ **Class** _____

Write in the spaces below an explanation of each term, based on what you learned and what you observed.

1. serve

2. set

3. forearm pass or bump

4. double hit

5. receiving team

6. legal hit

7. sideout

56

Identifying Shapes Musically

Peggy Tordoff • Kindergarten Teacher • Pineville, LA

Student Objectives

Students will be able to:
- develop a sense of rhythm and rhyme.
- use music as an aid to recall information.
- classify objects according to shape.
- identify five of the basic plane geometric shapes.
- work independently to reproduce shapes.

Materials Needed

Teacher:
- song lyrics, printed below
- knowledge of tune to "My Darling Clementine"

Students:
- "Identifying Shapes Musically" worksheet
- scissors
- pencil

New Terminology

circle: rounded, enclosed figure, having no sides or corners

square: figure having four equal sides and corners

triangle: figure having three sides and three corners

rectangle: figure having four sides (two long and two short) and four corners

diamond: figure having four diagonal sides and four corners

Lesson Activity Process

Clock 25–30 minutes.
The teacher will:
1. Ask students to identify shapes in the classroom environment. (Examples include the rectangle top of desk, the circle top of wastebasket, etc.)
2. For older children, explain the difference between plane geometric shapes (circle, square) and solid geometric shapes (sphere, cube).
3. Draw the following plane geometric shapes on the chalkboard: circle, square, rectangle, triangle, diamond. While drawing each shape, sing, or have a volunteer sing, the corresponding verse from the following song:

"Shapes"
(Sung to the tune of "Oh My Darling Clementine")

I'm a circle, I'm a circle, I'm a circle, round and fat.
I have no sides or corners.
Now what do you think of that?

I'm a square, I'm a square, I'm a square. That's my name.
I have four corners,
And my sides are all the same.

I'm a rectangle, I'm a rectangle, I'm a rectangle. I'm wide.
I am almost like a square,
But I have two long sides.

I'm a triangle, I'm a triangle, I'm a triangle. That's me.
You can count my sides and corners.
Here they are now—1, 2, 3.

I'm a diamond, I'm a diamond, and a diamond is so bright.
I have four sides and corners,
And I look just like a kite.

Now you know all these shapes.
None of them are just the same.
And when I point to each one,
You can tell me that shape's name.

4. Have the students identify the shapes when you point to them.
5. Have the students sing the song with you while they draw each shape in the air. Younger students also can work in groups of three or four to create shapes with their bodies (lying on the floor) for each verse.
6. Now distribute the "Identifying Shapes Musically" worksheets. Have younger students use their scissors to cut along the dotted lines. Older students can tear along the dotted lines.
7. As a class, sing the song again, one verse at a time. With each verse, direct younger students to draw and cut out the corresponding shape in the appropriate worksheet box. Older students should, without first drawing, tear each shape out of the correct box.

57

8. With all five shapes in front of them, ask students to hold up the corresponding shapes as they sing the song again.

Modifications for Students with Special Needs
- Instead of holding up the cutout shapes, have students point to the correct shapes on the chalkboard.
- Have a peer helper cut or tear shapes.
- Use larger squares for the cutout shapes.

Evaluation
The teacher should observe the ability of each student to:
- sing about musical shapes.
- identify shapes.
- create shapes by cutting or tearing.
  NOTE: Exact shapes and accurate proportions are not expected.

Answers to Student Worksheet
At the conclusion of the lesson, each student should have created the following "approximate" shapes by cutting or tearing the handout into five sections—circle, square, rectangle, triangle, and diamond.

Tips for Success
- Be aware of the need to render individual assistance during the drawing and cutting or tearing activities. Younger children especially may need considerable modeling and guiding for these processes.
- Rough approximations of the shapes are acceptable.

Notes for Next Time

- You may wish to conduct this activity as a cooperative learning situation. Students could be paired, placed in small groups, or work individually to produce shapes.
- The objective of this lesson is primarily to learn and enjoy singing the song. Take care to preserve the "fun" element of the activity while still guiding the task of identifying and producing shapes.

Additional Related Activities
1. Students can use parts of the body (fingers, arms, etc.) to create shapes as each verse is sung.
2. If floor space allows, younger students can walk around the room in the pattern of each shape as the verses are sung. Older students can stand together to form the shapes.
3. With older students, explain the difference between plane geometric shapes (figures having only two dimensions, such as width and height) and solid geometric shapes (figures having three dimensions, such as width, height, and depth). Now distribute pieces of paper (recycled paper is fine), and ask students to create a solid geometric shape. Students can do this simply by crushing the paper to form a sphere. Or students can experiment with cutting and folding a piece of paper to produce a cube or pyramid.
4. With upper grades, ask students to name additional shapes (like hexagon, trapezoid) and try to write a verse to the song using the new shape names.

Identifying Shapes Musically

Name _____   Date _____ Class _____

Tear or cut this sheet along the dotted lines to form five separate sections.

Tear or cut each section to resemble the designated shape.

59

Art

Manipulating Space

Micheal Gold-Vukson • Elementary Art Teacher • Lafayette, IN

Student Objectives

Students will be able to:

- discuss similarities and differences between two-dimensional and three-dimensional spaces.
- develop volume and area by creating a three-dimensional paper sculpture.

Materials Needed

Teacher:

- ruler or yardstick

Students:

- pencil
- construction paper or white paper (recycled paper is fine)
- scissors
- paste, glue, or glue sticks

New Terminology

dimension: a measure in one direction

two-dimensional space: space taken up by something with measurements in two directions

three-dimensional space: space taken up by something with measurements in three directions

Lesson Activity Process

Clock 25–35 minutes.

The teacher will:

1. Draw a straight line on the chalkboard and ask a volunteer to measure the line. The volunteer should take a ruler and announce how many inches in length. Tell students that when you measure the line, you only need to determine one measurement. The line has only one dimension—length.

2. Now get out a sheet of paper, and ask a volunteer to measure the paper. Point out that, to measure the paper, the volunteer will take two measurements, length and width. The paper is two-dimensional.

3. Ask a volunteer to use a ruler to measure an eraser. Ask the students what measurements the volunteer will have to take in order to measure the eraser. Students should answer length, height, and width. Explain that anything that needs three measurements is three-dimensional.

4. Ask students to identify things around the room that are two-dimensional (students might indicate the chalkboard, wall posters, homework papers, etc.). Now ask them to identify three-dimensional objects (desks, chairs, the tissue box, the clock, etc.).

5. Have a volunteer distribute paper to the class. Tell students they are going to perform magic. They are going to take a two-dimensional piece of paper and transform it into a three-dimensional object. (For younger students, you may wish to have them first follow your example as you fold a piece of paper to create three-dimensional accordion pleats.) Tell students that their assignment is to create the biggest three-dimensional object they can out of one two-dimensional sheet of paper. Students can cut, paste, or fold the paper in any way they choose.

6. Ask students to display their completed paper sculptures. Lead a discussion in which students talk about the thought processes they used to determine how to proceed.

Modifications for Students with Special Needs

- Provide examples, such as a cylinder or accordion pleats, that students can duplicate.
- Have a peer helper create the three-dimensional object by following the instructions of the special needs student.

Evaluation

Have students autograph their three-dimensional sculptures and collect them. Evaluate the completed three-dimensional shapes by asking students to identify the most unusual shape, the tallest and biggest sculptures, the most stable sculpture, and one(s) created without glue (or without cutting).

Tips for Success

- Remember that, for this activity, the aesthetic value of the shapes created by the students is not important.
- Circulate during work time to offer suggestions and observe how students manipulate the paper to enclose space.
- Make sure students have enough time to complete their three-dimensional shapes.
- Allow students to evaluate their own completed projects verbally.

Notes for Next Time

Additional Related Activities

1. For more colorful sculptures, have students color one side of the paper before beginning their shapes.
2. Ask students to use a piece of paper to create the smallest three-dimensional object they can.
3. Divide the class into pairs and have each pair of students use two pieces of paper together to create a three-dimensional object.
4. Ask students to identify the biggest three-dimensional object in the class.

Predicting What's in the Box

Donna M. Viveiros • Grade 6 Teacher • Fall River, MA

Critical Thinking

Student Objectives

Students will be able to:
- integrate language development with thinking skills.
- work together as a group to brainstorm ideas.
- think critically in order to predict, reason, and inquire.

Materials Needed

Teacher:
- one large bag of M&M's
- a box (no bigger than a shoe box)
- *optional:* wrapping paper, ribbon, and a bow

Students:
- "Predicting What's in the Box" worksheet
- pencil

New Terminology

brainstorming: a group working together to come up with as many ideas as possible without yet judging how "good" they are

Lesson Activity Process

Clock 20–25 minutes.
The teacher will:
1. Before class begins, and out of the sight of students, put the bag of M&M's in the box and wrap the box as if it were a present. Put the wrapped box on display in front of the class.
2. Tell students they are going to play a game called "What's in the Box?" First, ask students to brainstorm, or think together, about what cannot be in the box. Record each answer on the chalkboard under the heading, "Couldn't Be." After listing all they can, ask students for the reason for each response. When students have finished responding, praise the class's brainstorming efforts.
3. Now that students have an idea of what cannot be in the box, divide the class into pairs and supply each pair with a copy of the worksheet. Ask each pair to brainstorm as many things as they can that they would like to be in the box. (For younger students, ask the pairs to draw pictures of at least four things they would like to see inside the box.)

4. Now ask each pair to tell its most creative or favorite answer. Write these answers on the chalkboard under the heading, "Could Be," and praise the class's creative thinking skills.
5. Pass the box quickly from student to student. When the box has been handled by all the students, direct students' attention to the list on the chalkboard under the heading, "Could Be." Go through the list one item at a time and ask students, based on what they now know, whether that item could be what is in the box. Cross out items on the list during the discussion. Ask, How did handling the box change your mind about what was inside? Ask students for any new ideas they might have about the box's contents.
6. Have a student open the box. Give each student some M&M's to celebrate the great job of brainstorming the class did. Avoid giving them to students who are allergic to chocolate.

Evaluation

Observation will determine whether students are working on task, in whole group, or with a partner. Each pair's worksheet also can be used as criterion for evaluation.

Modifications for Students with Special Needs

- Rather than ask a student with cognitive delays to think spontaneously of answers, give choices first. For example, "Could what's in the box be a pig or a jelly bean?" "Could it be a button or a house?" Then ask the learner for a new guess.
- Have a peer helper write down student's suggestions.
- Provide other clues to what is in the box, i.e., direct students to think about smell, shape, sounds, etc.

Tips for Success

- Set up clear rules of behavior prior to the activity.
- Give sufficient time for students to think and respond.
- Have all needed materials—the wrapped box and the worksheets—prepared and waiting for distribution; searching for materials can interrupt a student's focus.

62

Additional Related Activities

1. If you are scheduled to spend more than one day in a classroom, give the students an assignment. Have them create their own "What's in the Bag?" Put students in cooperative groups of four to share and solve their mystery bag with peers, using one or all of the procedures used with "What's in the Box?" (With younger students, whole-group sharing is best.

    Kindergarten and first-grade students can give the initial letter of what's in their bag for brainstorming.)

2. Lead a discussion in which students talk about presents whose contents they guessed before the presents were opened. Ask, How did you know ahead of time what was in the box?

Notes for Next Time

63

Predicting What's in the Box?

Name _____   Date _____ Class _____

Time limit: 5 minutes

Your assignment is to brainstorm with a partner what you would like to see in the box. Try to come up with as many answers as possible. Record your answers in the space below. If you need more room, use the back of this paper. Count them and record your number. You have five minutes for this activity.

What I/we would like to see in the box

Number of items

Middle School Lesson Activities

What Is a Middle School?

During your early adolescent years, you may have attended a junior high school instead of a middle school. Middle schools are the most recent form of school organization in the United States, though it should be noted that some middle schools have assumed the name but primarily function as traditional "junior" high schools. Intended to help ease students' transition between elementary school and high school, middle schools are designed to meet the special needs of 10- to 14-year-old students. Some middle schools consist of grades 5–8; others contain grades 7–8. However, the majority of middle schools include grades 6–8.

Characteristics of middle schools include teacher teaming, student advisory programs, flexible block scheduling, and exploratory curriculum. Teacher teams are generally organized around the core subject areas—math, science, language arts, and social studies. Each team of teachers has the same 125 students during the course of the day. These teachers are able to share knowledge about and concern for these students and to plan their curriculum together. Teacher teams may plan interdisciplinary units of study around common themes, helping students to see the connections between various disciplines. Teacher teams may also coordinate the scheduling of major tests, homework policies, and classroom rules. These coordination efforts aid students in adjusting to school beyond the elementary level. With flexible scheduling, teams may decide to allocate blocks of time to special projects and activities. For example, on a particular day two class periods may be devoted to a science lab rather than the usual one period. Teams may also combine classes for field trips and guest speakers.

Advisory programs are similar to the junior high school's homeroom concept except that more attention is given to each student's personal development.

65

Chapter 6

Teachers and other school personnel are assigned small groups of students with whom they meet on a regular basis to discuss study skills, interpersonal skills, and career guidance. Additionally, an exploratory curriculum facilitates students' personal development by providing a common "wheel" of experiences. Every 6- or 9-week period, students investigate a different area of study, such as music, art, keyboarding, foreign language, and/or health. Exploratory courses help students examine new areas of learning and begin making career decisions.

In general, the middle school is more like an elementary school than a high school. While students may change classes as in high school, a special effort is made for at least one adult to know each student well, providing assistance as early adolescents leave elementary school and prepare to enter high school.

What Are Middle School Students Like?

Middle school students present a wide range of variability. Some may resemble older students due to their tall stature, while others may look more like children. The rate of physical maturation that takes place during this time is only surpassed by that of a two-year-old. Keep in mind that girls are usually two years ahead of boys in terms of these physical changes. Add to the physical transformation the process of sexual maturation and it is no wonder that young adolescents invest much psychic energy adjusting to such overwhelming changes!

Young adolescents are concerned about their physical and sexual development—or lack thereof—and often it becomes a central theme in their lives. Thus, it is quite normal that early adolescents become so preoccupied with their physical development that they believe others are always watching them. Seemingly trivial matters—to us—are major sources of worry to early adolescents. They are especially sensitive about the clumsiness caused by their uneven growth patterns. Middle school students are very self-conscious about their physical changes, so teachers at this level should not call attention to these differences and should

protect young adolescents' need for privacy. Moreover, teachers should provide opportunities for stretching and moving around in the classroom to meet these students' needs for physical activity.

Although they may present a facade of toughness, middle school students' feelings are easily hurt. The emotional roller coaster that early adolescents seem to ride is a thrilling one as emotions increase in intensity. Young adolescents may often lose themselves in love, fear, or anger. Their fear of being ridiculed or ostracized by peers is a main concern. Saving face becomes a critical issue for them. To embarrass a middle school student in front of his or her peers is to damage the trust relationship that is so important in teaching.

Seeking a personal identity and becoming independent are the primary tasks of early adolescence. As middle school students seek to find their place, the peer group has much power. Swayed by what others think, early adolescents do not dare to be different. Being accepted by peers is of paramount importance. Even though they desire to be independent of adults, early adolescents are ambivalent about their emerging responsibilities. One day they may want to be given much freedom, and the next day they may demand coddling.

Intellectually, middle school students are best described as transitional thinkers, because more are moving from concrete levels of thinking to abstract levels as greater reasoning powers emerge. Because of their ability to imagine possibilities and to visualize the ideal, early adolescents become critical of others, especially adults. They are intensely curious, particularly about themselves and relationships, and they become more introspective because of their ability to think about thinking.

As a result of their heightened sensitivity and new cognitive abilities, middle school students are keenly aware of fairness issues. Teachers should respect this need for fair treatment in their interactions with young adolescents. Knowing that middle school students desire structure and clear limits, teachers should make their expectations explicit. To facilitate their growing independence, teachers can also provide choices.

What Responsibilities Might You Have?

As a substitute teacher in a middle school, you may find yourself in a variety of roles. You may be expected to chaperone a field trip, serve as an advisor during an abbreviated advisory period, collect forms and/or money, provide supervision (pull "duty") in the cafeteria or the hallway, or monitor the restrooms. Talk with other team teachers regularly. If you are substituting for one teacher on an extended basis, you may be expected to attend team planning meetings. Successful middle school substitutes have the same skills as the regular teachers—they are flexible, sensitive to the needs of early adolescents, provide creative outlets for students' expression of their feelings, project warmth, and show genuine enthusiasm for teaching at this level.

In the remainder of this chapter you will find several lesson plans developed by middle school teachers. Use these examples as guides to develop your own plans or to modify existing ones. In general, here are some practical teaching tips to follow:

1. Provide variety in your lessons. Never attempt to do the same thing for the entire class period. Middle school students will lose interest.

2. Write assignments and page numbers on the board or overhead projector. Do not just announce them orally. Students need visual as well as auditory reminders.

3. Learn the students' names. Get to know them as individuals.

4. Circulate among students to answer their questions and to offer encouragement. Don't just sit at the teacher's desk.

5. Provide opportunities for peer contact. Telling students, "Turn to your neighbor and share answers or opinions," is an effective technique that promotes interaction.

6. Use the newspaper as a teaching resource in order to make lessons more relevant to students. For example, sale advertisements on products of interest to early adolescents—e.g., CDs, athletic shoes, videos—can be used to reinforce math skills.

7. Listen and empathize. Don't make light of students' concerns and anxieties. Remember what your early adolescent period of development was like. If you have forgotten, there may be a reason!

6–8 Identifying Kinds of Writing

Language Arts

Griselle M. Diaz-Gemmati • Grades 7–8 Teacher • Chicago, IL

Student Objectives

Students will be able to:
- apply information from a short story to another writing format.
- identify different kinds of writing.

Materials Needed

Teacher:
- scissors
- several photocopies of the "Identifying Kinds of Writing" worksheet
- a short story of a length not to exceed 10 minutes when read to the class (from the students' literature text or the school library)

Students:
- slips of the "Identifying Kinds of Writing" worksheet
- pencil
- paper

68

New Terminology

fable: a story with a moral that teaches a lesson

Lesson Activity Process

Clock 1 hour.

The teacher will:

1. Run several photocopies of the worksheet and ask volunteers to cut the photocopies into strips. Fold the strips and put them in a hat or a bag. (NOTE: If you do not have access to a photocopy machine, you can have students pick a number between one and nine; students' assignment will be the corresponding number on the handout.)

2. Read aloud, or have students take turns reading aloud, the short story you have chosen. (Students may also be able to help with this choice.) Discuss the kind of writing this selection is. Then walk up and down the aisles with the hat, allowing each student to reach in and pull out a paper strip. Tell students they are to complete the writing task on the paper strip in about 75 words, based on information they heard from the story.

3. When students have finished their writing assignments, ask volunteers to share their compositions

with the class. Then ask the class how the information in one composition differed from another, based on the writing assignment (news story, fable, advertisement, etc.).

Modifications for Students with Special Needs

- Have the student write down, as a list, the events of the short story the class read together.
- Have the student type the assignment on a typewriter or computer or dictate their assignments into a tape recorder or dictaphone.
- Have a peer helper write down the story for the student.

Evaluation

Compare each student's completed writing assignment to the task. Also note whether individual students listened attentively during the short-story reading.

Tips for Success

- Choose a short story no longer than a couple of pages to maintain student interest. You may wish to have students identify their favorite short story from their English book, or a story in their English book that they have not yet read.
- Select a story with strong characters and a hero or heroine to match several of the writing tasks on the worksheet.
- Allow ample writing time for the students. You may need to adjust the 75-word count based on the available time.
- Additional writing styles can be tailored to a specific short story. For example, if the short story has an animal, one writing assignment could be to have students imagine they are the animal and write the story from the animal's point of view.

Additional Related Activities

1. List on the chalkboard the steps many successful authors use when writing—outline, rough draft, revision, peer review, final draft, presentation or publication. Ask students to explain what they think happens at every step.

2. Divide the class into pairs, and direct the students in each pair to read their compositions to their partners. Partners then should make suggestions for a final draft. Remind students that their assignment is to help, not criticize, their partners' work.
3. Provide examples of some of the kinds of writing students have been practicing in this activity. For example, read a newspaper article and ask students to determine whether the article answers the journalistic questions of who, what, when, where, why, and how.
4. Review with the students the kinds of writing identified in this activity. Then, as each student presents his or her work, have the class guess what type of writing the presenter was assigned.

Notes for Next Time

Identifying Kinds of Writing

1. Imagine that you work for an advertising agency. Write an ad of no more than 75 words that would encourage other students to read this story.

- -

2. Imagine that you are a literature reviewer. Write a 75-word essay that critiques the story you just read. Tell whether you would recommend this story to others.

- -

3. Imagine you are going to give an award to the nicest person in the story. Write a 75-word paragraph explaining whom you would choose and why.

- -

4. Imagine you are a screenwriter. Write a 75-word scene from an imaginary movie script in which two of the story's characters have a conversation.

- -

5. Imagine you are a guest at the home of the hero or heroine. Write a personal letter of no more than 75 words to a friend describing the house.

- -

6. Use the characters in this story to write a 75-word fable. Remember that a fable has a moral that teaches a lesson.

- -

7. Imagine you are a journalist whose assignment is to write a 75-word newspaper article on the events of this story. Remember that newspaper articles try to answer these questions—who, what, when, where, why, and how.

- -

8. Imagine you are the hero or heroine of this story. Write a 75-word diary entry that tells what happens in your own words. Don't forget to talk about how the events affected you.

- -

9. Write a poem of no more than 75 words about the story you have just read. Your poem can be about events or about one particular character.

6-8 Creating a Planet

Composition

Lynda Hatch • Assistant Professor • Flagstaff, AZ

Student Objectives

Students will be able to:

- tell the difference between scientific information and science fiction.
- combine science with fiction to write a piece of science fiction.

Materials Needed

Students:

- paper
- pencil
- crayons or markers

New Terminology

science fiction: fiction that deals with the influence of real or imagined science on society or individuals

(Depending on their backgrounds, students might need clarification regarding what defines a planet as compared to stars, asteroids, comets, meteors, meteorites, and the like. In that case, the following definitions might come in handy.)

planet: a heavenly body other than a comet, asteroid, or satellite that travels in orbit around the sun

star: a hot, rotating, ball-shaped, gaseous heavenly body (like the sun, our nearest star) of great mass that shines by its own light through nuclear fusion reactions in its core

asteroid: one of thousands of small rocky chunks, or "minor planets," between Mars and Jupiter each having a diameter ranging in size from a fraction of a kilometer to nearly 800 kilometers

comet: a bright heavenly body made up of ice, frozen gas, and dust that develops a long, shining tail as it moves around the sun in a long oval orbit

meteor: one of the small bodies of matter in the solar system observable when it falls into the earth's atmosphere where the heat of friction causes it to glow brightly for a short time but burn up before it reaches the ground (also called a "shooting star" though it is not really a star)

meteorite: a meteor that crashes into the surface of the earth, moon, or other heavenly body

Lesson Activity Process

Clock 45–50 minutes.

The teacher will:

1. Ask students, "What is science fiction?" Then ask them to name their favorite science fiction writers.

2. Emphasize to the students that science fiction goes beyond what we have experienced but that what started as science fiction may indeed become reality. For example, submarines were invented long after Jules Verne imagined them in his book *20,000 Leagues under the Sea*. The book *Journey to the Moon* imagined traveling to the moon long before that trip became scientifically possible.

3. Tell students that some science fiction books deal with future on Earth, but other books create whole new planets, where everything is new and strange. Ask students to imagine they are science fiction writers. What would they have to consider when creating their new world? Student answers should include what the land looks like, what the living creatures look like, what kind of government is in place there, etc. Write student suggestions on the chalkboard.

4. Have students look out the window and describe the landscape of planet Earth. Then lead a discussion in which students work together as a class to create a new landscape for a new planet. Write their ideas down on the chalkboard. Basic questions should be answered as students discuss their new landscape. Are there mountains? Deserts? Plains? Water? Tropics? Ice caps? Islands? Volcanoes? Oceans? What is the climate like? How many suns are in the sky? How many moons?

5. Once students have fleshed out a landscape, divide the class into pairs and give each pair two pieces of paper. Tell students that their job is to describe a living creature that inhabits this imaginary planet. Remind them that the life they "create" needs to be compatible with the landscape the class imagined.

6. Once the pair has discussed a creature, have one member write a paragraph describing the creature while the other member draws a picture of the creature.

7. Ask the pairs of students to share their creations with the class. Then ask students how all these creatures would interact with each other on this new planet.

Modifications for Students with Special Needs

- Allow students to use a typewriter or computer to write their paragraphs.
- Have students record their creature descriptions on a tape recorder or dictaphone.
- Assign a peer tutor to write for the student.

Evaluation

Read the written descriptions and examine the pictures for detail. Also consider student's participation in the landscape discussion.

Notes for Next Time

Tips for Success

- Ask the school librarian for a small collection of science fiction books, and show students their covers or inside illustrations as inspiration for the lesson.
- Remind students that the creatures they create should be appropriate for a school assignment.

Additional Related Activities

1. If you know you will be returning to the class for several days, or if you discover students who have been especially excited by this lesson, you may wish to have students create the setting to their own science fiction books. Distribute the "Creating a Planet" worksheet and review the directions with students. Put completed books, with their authors' permission, on display for the class to enjoy.
2. Science fiction is certainly not restricted simply to topics related to universe science. Students could read books, write, and discuss other types of science fiction, such as living under the ocean or futuristic cities on earth, even romance science fiction.

Creating a Planet

Name _____ Date _____ Class _____

To Make Your Book: Fold 5 pieces of paper in half. Stitch or staple the pages
together to form a 20-page book. Number the pages.

To Write Your Book: The first thing you'll need to do is name your planet. Then
write/draw the following things on each page, in the order listed. You do
not have to address all of the points—they are just to give you ideas. You
may think of other things you want to include.

Contents of Your Book

Page 1. Front cover—Tell the name of the planet and draw
a colored picture.

Page 2. Inside front cover—Leave it blank or add your
own publishing information.

Page 3. Title page—Tell the name of your planet, your
name, and the date. Draw a colored picture that
illustrates your planet.

Page 4. Draw and color a detailed picture of the landscape
of your planet. Write the word "Landscape" at the
bottom of the page.

Page 5. Draw and color a detailed picture of the people or
creatures that live on your planet. Write the word
"Life" at the bottom of the page.

Page 6. Write a description of what the land looks like—
mountains, deserts, plains, precipitation, tropics, ice
caps, islands, volcanoes, oceans, weather, cities,
atmosphere.

Page 7. Write a description of the vegetation—plants,
flowers, trees, bacteria, jungles.

Page 8. Write a description of the people (or creatures)—
size, color, shape, personality, religion, clothing, shoes,
body parts like eyes and ears and hair.

Page 9. Write a description of the animals—types, colors,
pets, animal homes, zoos, predator/prey relationships, camouflage.

Page 10. Write a description of the government (how the
planet is ruled)—president, dictator, voting, military,
crime, jails, courts, laws, states and countries, flag.

Page 11. Write a description of transportation—cars,
planes, subways, rockets to other planets, flying

saucers, trains, traffic laws, streets/freeways.

Page 12. Write a description of the schools—architecture,
setup of a classroom, playgrounds, subjects studied,
school lunches, reform schools, report cards, homework, colleges, school supplies, teachers/principals,
length of school day/year.

Page 13. Write a description of the planet's economics—
money, banks, bank robbers, rich/poor people.

Page 14. Write a description of what the creatures do in
their leisure (free) time—games, sports, camps,
hobbies, bikes, youth groups like Scouts, television,
music, art, books, dances.

Page 15. Write a description of manufacturing and
farming—how the parents make a living, child labor
laws, types of crops and farm animals, industry,
pollution, foods they produce, land-use planning.

Page 16. Write a description of their past history—
invasions by other planets, peacetime, their experience with Earth, their future, their heroes and hero-
ines.

Page 17. About the Author page—Write a description of
yourself as the author of this book. Do not write in
first person. Add a colored picture or a colored
border.

Page 18. Comments page—Get the positive comments of
at least two people (one must be an adult—a parent or
guardian). Add a colored picture or a colored border.

Page 19. Inside back cover—leave it blank.

Page 20. Outside back cover—leave it blank or repeat your
publishing company's name and logo.

73

Interpreting Tables

Patricia Powell • Grade 6 Teacher • Chattanooga, TN

Student Objectives

Students will be able to:

- solve problems by organizing data into a table.
- learn the importance of displaying results of school surveys, votes, and grades in a table or graph.
- practice cooperative learning to construct a table.

Materials Needed

Students:

- pencil
- paper
- ruler
- "Interpreting Tables" worksheet

New Terminology

statistics: a branch of mathematics that deals with the collection, presentation, and analysis of numerically presented data

tally sheet: a sheet on which data are summarized by recording points or marks

frequency table: a table that illustrates the number of times an event occurs

Lesson Activity Process

Clock 45–55 minutes.

The teacher will:

1. Begin the lesson by asking students to name their favorite places to eat. Call on students randomly, and list their responses on board. Limit to 4–6 popular responses.

2. Ask the students how they might find out which restaurants are most popular among their classmates. Then explain that the class will use the mathematics of statistics (define the term) to determine the class's favorite restaurant.

3. Draw a three-columned table on the board or the overhead projector. At the top of the first column, write "Name of Restaurant." The second column should be titled "Tally," while the third column should have the heading "Frequency."

4. Have a student volunteer enter in the first column the restaurant names the students provided.

5. Now have each student come to the board and put a mark in the "Tally" column next to his or her favorite restaurant. Remind students they may vote for no more than one restaurant.

6. After each student has made a selection, have a volunteer add the marks by each restaurant and put each restaurant's total in the "Frequency" column. Ask the class, "Which restaurant is most frequently named as the favorite?"

7. Distribute copies of the "Interpreting Tables" worksheet to the class. Tell students they have five minutes to complete the worksheet. When five minutes are up, discuss worksheet answers as a class.

8. Now tell students they are to use a blank piece of paper, a ruler, and a pencil to construct a frequency table that will show the frequency of student birth dates by month. When their tables are ready, have students call out in rows the months of their birthdays, emphasizing that they must listen carefully and make a tally mark on their tables for all the other students. Students then should complete the other two columns of their frequency tables. When they have finished, ask students to compare their answers with the answers of the other students.

9. Finish the lesson by leading a discussion in which students talk about what other kinds of information could be illustrated using a frequency table.

Modifications for Students with Special Needs

- Construct the birth date table as a class, rather than individually.
- Have students file by the student's desk, making their tally marks (rather than the special needs student walking around the room).
- Pair students with peer helpers.

Evaluation

Birth-date frequency tables can be collected and used for evaluation purposes. If you wish, you can assign bonus points to students who complete their tables quietly.

Answers to Student Handout

1. 80–89
2. 16 (you may need to point out that this answer would include two categories—90–100 and 80–89)
3. 11 (you may need to point out that this answer would include two categories—70–79 and Below 70)
4. Answers may vary but should indicate that the data are easier to look at and interpret, etc.
5. Answers may vary (groups of five make it easier for you to count your tallies with hundreds to add up)

Tips for Success

- Walk around the room as students are completing their worksheets and tables, making sure that the basic concepts of this lesson are individually understood.
- For those who have difficulty with the concept of a frequency table, help students construct and complete other frequency tables, using topics suggested by the students. Topics could include the class's favorite singing group or favorite song, the class's favorite sport or television show, etc.

Notes for Next Time

Additional Related Activities

1. Distribute recent newspapers and ask students to determine whether any tables used are frequency tables. Tell students that line graphs, bar graphs, and picture graphs all started as frequency tables. Have students identify the topics of each frequency table.
2. Distribute graph paper and have students use the information from their own frequency tables to construct a bar graph.
3. Challenge accelerated math students by having them determine fractions for each number in the table's "Frequency" column.

75

Interpreting Frequency Tables

Name _____ **Date** _____ **Class** _____

Mrs. Powell completed grading the Unit Test on fractions. To see how well the classes performed, Mrs. Powell made a frequency table for each period that showed each student's test scores. One of the classes is listed below.

Fourth Period's Scores

Interval	Tally	Frequency
90–100	|||||		6
80–89	||||| |||||	10
70–79	||||| |||	8
Below 70	|||	3

1. Between which scores did the greatest number of Mrs. Powell's students fall? _____

2. How many students received scores of 80 or better on their math tests? _____

3. How many students' scores fell below 80? _____

4. Why is it important to organize data? _____

_____

5. Why are tallies usually shown in groups of 5? _____

_____

Conducting an Experiment

Dixie Carpenter • Grade 7 Science Teacher • Glendale, AZ

Student Objectives

The students will be able to:
- answer the question: How many drops of water will fit on a penny?
- observe and define surface tension.
- review the six parts of a laboratory experiment.

Materials Needed

Teacher:
- several pennies
- one or two eye droppers
- paper towels
- paper cup

Students:
- "Conducting an Experiment" worksheet
- "Wordsearch" handout
- paper
- pencil

New Terminology

surface tension: a force that causes the surface of liquids to behave in certain ways, for example, to cause water drops to take a spherical shape.

Students should review the steps scientists follow when performing an experiment:

problem: the question scientists are trying to answer in an experiment

hypothesis: a possible answer to the question

materials: items necessary to perform an experiment

procedure: steps followed in the experiment

observations: what students see, smell, hear, taste, or feel

conclusion: results of the experiment

Lesson Activity Process

Clock 45–55 minutes.

The teacher will:

1. Before the activity begins, write the following words on the chalkboard: Problem; Hypothesis; Materials; Procedure; and Observations.

2. Tell students that they are going to do an experiment to find out how many drops of water can fit on a penny. Point out that the words on the board will help them conduct a successful experiment. Ask, What is the problem? What are some hypotheses regarding how many drops will fit on the penny? What materials will we need to conduct this experiment? What procedures should we follow?

3. Divide the class into pairs, and distribute copies of the word search handout. Explain that, as pairs of students come to the desk to perform the experiment, the other students should create their own word searches. Word search words should include the materials and scientific steps listed on the board. You may want to underline words to be included.

4. Distribute the "Conducting an Experiment" worksheet to each pair.

5. On a desk in the front of the room, place a penny head-side up on a paper towel, and fill the cup with water. Invite students, in pairs, to the desk to conduct the experiment. Students should bring their worksheets with them. For each pair, demonstrate how to drop the water onto the penny and offer hints for getting the maximum number of drops on the penny—for example, don't hold the dropper so high water will splatter or so low that the dropper touches the top of water. Remind students to form a hypothesis about how many drops of water will fit. Students should write their hypotheses on their worksheets before proceeding with the experiment.

6. Have one student use the eyedropper to place water, one drop at a time, on the penny. Have the other student in the pair count the number of drops and record it on the worksheet (the number of drops can vary from 60 to over 250). Remind students to observe the penny from the side so they can draw what they see, a question on their worksheets. Students should return to their seats to complete the remainder of the worksheet and to work on their word searches.

7. When all pairs have completed the experiment, have them call out how many drops they successfully placed on the penny's head. Write down all the numbers in a list and ask a volunteer to add them up. Divide by the number of pairs of students to find the average number of drops.

8. Lead a discussion in which students talk about what they learned. Ask students why so many drops fit on the penny's head. Then explain the concept of surface

tension. Ask how this experiment is an illustration of that scientific concept.

Modifications for Students with Special Needs

- Assign the student to do the counting while the partner handles the eyedropper.
- Orally discuss the results, rather than requiring a formal write-up.

Evaluation

Compare students' completed worksheets with the answers listed below.

Answers to Student Handout

Problem: How many drops of water can fit on the head of a penny?

Hypothesis: Any guess regarding the number of water drops is acceptable

Materials: penny, paper towel, paper cup, eye dropper, water

Procedure:
1. Place penny on paper towel.
2. Fill cup with water.
3. Use eye dropper to place one water drop at a time on the penny.
4. Observe water on penny and draw what you see.

Observation: Students should write down the number of water drops they actually placed on the penny's head. Students also should draw what they saw when they observed the penny from the side.

Conclusion: Students should write down the class's average number of drops and explain how this experiment is an illustration of surface tension.

Notes for Next Time

Tips for Success

- If students are working effectively, you may wish to set up two experiment sites and allow two pairs of students to work simultaneously.
- To avoid arguments, determine who will assume each role by having the students count off by twos. Number one drops the water on the penny and number two records the information. Name them the experimenter and the observer and stress the importance of both roles.
- If you have more than one class, you may find that the afternoon classes will get many more drops of water on the penny because they have heard the conversations and tips of students who already performed the experiment.
- You may wish to have students write down the number of drops each pair discovered, then add the total number for the class. Then have a volunteer check the addition with a calculator.
- If you are not able to make photocopies, have students use the back of a piece of paper to create their own word search worksheets. Tell them to use rulers and pencils to construct a grid with 18 squares across the page and 18 squares down the side.

Additional Related Activities

1. Have students exchange and complete each other's word search worksheets.
2. The experiment could be replicated on the other side of the penny. Ask students to guess whether more drops of water will fit on the penny's tail side or head side (the answer is tail). Nickels, dimes, and quarters also can be used.
3. Conduct a "Drop-Off" competition in which all pairs of students who were able to place more than 200 drops on the penny compete against each other. The winning pair is the one with the most water drops on the penny.

Conducting an Experiment

Name _____ **Date** _____ **Class** _____

1. Problem

2. Hypothesis

3. Materials

1.

2.

3.

4.

4. Procedure

Step 1

Step 2

Step 3

Step 4

Step 5

5. Observations

In the box below, draw a side view of the penny with water on it.

6. Conclusion

_____ drops of water fit on my penny. This is _____ than my original hypothesis. I think so many drops fit because _____

_____

_____

Conducting an Experiment

Name _____ **Date** _____ **Class** _____

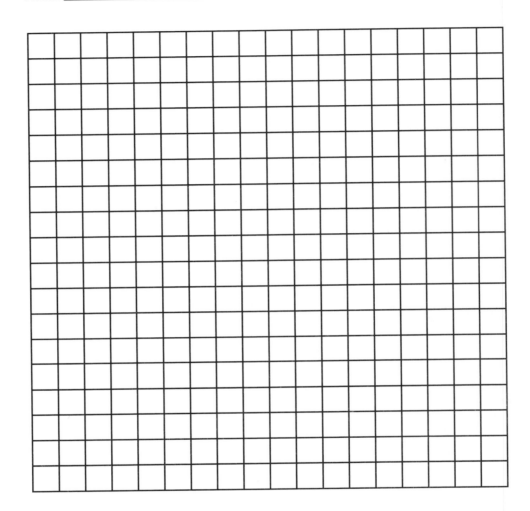

Understanding Population Density

Connie J. Dwyer • Grade 7 Teacher • London, OH

Social Studies

Student Objectives

Students will be able to:
- work effectively in groups.
- define population density.
- formulate opinions about world overcrowding.

Materials Needed

Teacher:
- four 2' x 2' squares of newsprint or chart paper
- overhead projector
- knowledge of the square mileage of the county in which students live

Students:
- their social studies textbook

New Terminology

population density: the number of people in a given area, usually stated as people per square mile or per square kilometer

Lesson Activity Process

Clock 45–55 minutes.

The teacher will:

1. Begin by asking students, In your home, do you have a bedroom to yourself, or do you share a bedroom? Do you feel you have enough space? How much room do you think you need in order to live comfortably? How much room would be too much room for one person?

2. Explain that many people who think about the future worry about overcrowding in the world. Ask students to guess how many people live in the world today. Write their guesses on the chalkboard. Then tell them that the answer is about 5.5 billion people.

3. Lay the four 2' x 2' newspaper squares together on the floor to form one 4' x 4' square. Tell students to imagine that it is really crowded in the room. Each person only has 4 square feet apiece. Now have four volunteers each stand on one of the newspaper squares. Volunteers should stand, hands on hips and elbows out, and slowly turn in a circle.

4. Tell students that what makes an area crowded or empty is its population density. In the example above, there are 4 people for every 16 square feet. This certainly would qualify as overcrowding. Now lead a discussion in which students guess the size of the area into which all the people of the world would fit if we stood in a group elbow-to-elbow. Would we need a continent's worth of land? Land the size of an ocean? You may wish to give clues, allowing students to revise their guesses after each clue. Say, "Everyone would fit on one continent. Everyone would fit on North America. Everyone would fit in the United States. Everyone would fit in one state."

5. Now tell students that, based upon a world population of 5.5 billion and a space of 4 square feet per person, everybody would fit in an area of only about 800 square miles! Compare this to the square miles of your county. This is similar in size to many midwestern U.S. counties. For example, Ohio's Franklin County, which includes the capital, Columbus, (540 sq. miles) plus half of neighboring Madison County (470 sq. miles) would accommodate the whole world's population!

6. Ask students to explain why, then, experts talk about overcrowding. (Student answers should indicate that people are not spread out evenly around the world.) Tell students that in some of the world's regions, the population density is less than 3 people per square mile. In other regions, population density reaches 3,000 people per square mile.

7. Divide the class into six groups and assign each group one of the following continents: Australia, Asia, Africa, Europe, North America, or South America. Tell the groups to locate their continents on maps in the back of their social studies books. Their assignment is to identify reasons why population is more dense in certain areas of the continent. (Groups should identify factors like the availability of rivers for fresh water and transportation, a temperate climate, etc.) Have the groups share their findings with the class.

8. Using information students have shared, lead a discussion in which students talk about what kinds of conditions encourage human settlement. Ask

students to explain why no group was assigned the continent of Antarctica.

Modifications for Students with Special Needs

- Have students point to a map, rather than responding verbally, to identify the world's most densely populated regions.
- Make a transparency of each map from the social studies textbook and place on the overhead projector, then make observations regarding reasons for population density as a class rather than in small groups.

Evaluation

Use class discussion and group participation as the basis for evaluation.

Tips for Success

- Point out to students that, although you measured population density of the paper squares in square feet, population density is usually measured in terms of square miles or square kilometers.
- Before the class breaks up for its group work, you may wish to display the social studies text maps on the overhead projector and ask students to identify the purpose of each map.
- Circulate among the groups as they work. Offer encouragement and clarify directions.

Notes for Next Time

Additional Related Activities

1. Integrate math activities with this social studies lesson. Tell students that everybody knows a billion is a lot. But how much exactly is a billion? Have students count off 10 seconds on the clock with you. Ask students to use paper and pencil to figure the following:
   a. How many seconds in one minute? (60)
   b. How many seconds in one hour? (60 x 60 = 3,600)
   c. How many seconds in one day? (3,600 x 24 = 86,400)
   d. How many seconds in one year? (86,400 x 365.25 = 31,557,600)
   e. How many years does it take to live 1 billion seconds? (31,557,600 x 31.7 = 1,000,375,900; the answer is a little over 31 and a half years)
   Remind students that Earth's population is over five times 1 billion.
2. Have students talk about ways people could make more of the Earth more livable, so that the population could spread out a little.
3. Working in groups, have students list problems they think may result from unequal population distribution and suggest solutions to these problems.
4. An excellent follow-up activity is one from Zero Population Growth, Inc. (1400 Sixteenth St. NW, Suite 320, Washington, D.C. 20036, 202–332–2200) called "Earth: The Apple of Our Eye." Write for a copy and place it in your survival kit. Students will discover that, although vast areas of our earth are almost unpopulated, the amount of arable land we have available to supply our food is quite small.

Analyzing Advertisements

Janet L. Henke • Grade 6–8 Mentor Teacher • Baltimore, MD
Russell G. Henke • Coordinator of Health Education • Rockville, MD

Student Objectives

Students will be able to:

- list advertising techniques used to sell health-care products.
- describe how consumers are influenced to buy health-care products.
- analyze advertisements based on the techniques and influences discussed in class.

Materials Needed

Teacher:

- magazine and newspaper clippings of health-care products ads

Students:

- pen or pencil
- "Analyzing Advertising" worksheet

New Terminology

Review with students the following advertising techniques used to gain consumer support:

bandwagon: the notion that everyone is using the product and, to be popular, the consumer needs it

empty promises: promising that the product will benefit the consumer

sex appeal: guaranteeing or suggesting that the product will make the consumer physically appealing to another

statistical: using numbers to convince the consumer that this product is the best

testimonial: emphasizing endorsements by others who state that the product worked for them

Lesson Activity Process

Clock 50 minutes.

The teacher will:

1. List the following health-care products on the chalkboard or on a transparency—toothpaste; shampoo; mouthwash; skin-care products; and deodorant.
2. Ask the students for examples from television, radio, billboards, magazines, or newspapers of advertisements for these products. Record the examples on the chalkboard next to the product listed.

3. Ask, How does each advertisement attempt to sell the product? For example, a mouthwash advertisement promises fresher, cleaner breath.
4. Distribute the "Analyzing Advertising" worksheet. Review the five advertising techniques with students, using the ads from the student list to illustrate each, if applicable.
5. Then ask students to divide into pairs and look through the ad clippings to list one or two examples of specific products for each of the five techniques on the handout.
6. Each pair should share its examples and explain how the advertisement illustrates that technique. Circulate in the classroom, assessing student progress.
7. After students are finished with the worksheet, ask the class to give two or three examples for each technique and describe how each illustrates that technique.
8. Ask students why these advertising techniques are used. Answers should include to sell the product; to sell more of the product than its competition; and to introduce a new product.
9. Assign students to write or draw an advertisement for a new health-care product for teens. The advertisement must use one or more of the five techniques discussed in class. If time allows, students can complete ad during class; if not, assign for homework.

Modifications for Students with Special Needs

- Match a peer helper with every student.
- Videotape the advertisements.
- Give ad examples by type and have student match the technique to the example

Evaluation

The student advertisement is presented to the class for peer review. Peers should match technique to each student ad. Criteria for evaluation should include creativity, accurate use of the technique, and neatness.

83

Answers to Student Handout

Students' answers and examples will vary according to the marketing strategies used in their area.

Tips for Success

- Prior to the lesson, collect school-appropriate magazines and newspapers that include examples of the advertising techniques to be discussed in the lesson. If time or opportunity permits, record advertisements from radio and television.
- When reviewing the worksheet with students, either read the explanations aloud or have a student volunteer read it aloud. Oral reading instead of silent reading will help focus students' attention.
- Allow time for discussion of each technique before moving to the next one.
- Some students may not be able to remember advertisements easily. The use of magazines and newspapers will enable them to complete the assignment.
- Make sure that students stay on task and that the examples that they are using relate to health-care products.
- Determine if the examples given by students accurately illustrate each technique. If an example given does not fit a particular technique, ask students what other technique it does reflect. Certain advertisements may use more than one technique.
- If time permits, the evaluation may be started in class or may be assigned as homework.

Additional Related Activities

1. Students could use the advertising techniques discussed in this lesson to analyze advertisements of other products such as tobacco, alcohol, nutrition, or clothing.
2. Encourage students to view television at home for 30 minutes and record the advertising techniques and examples they see during that time.
3. Students could make a poster or collage of advertisements that illustrate one technique.

Notes for Next Time

Analyzing Advertising

Name _____ **Date** _____ **Class** _____

Find an ad that illustrates each of the following advertising techniques. Write the product name and the claim made about the product that indicates the technique used.

Bandwagon: This technique attempts to convince the consumer that everyone is using a particular product. To be popular, the consumer needs this product.
Example: A deodorant advertisement may show a user who is very popular and hint that you will be popular if you use this deodorant.
Student's Example

Empty Promises: This technique falsely promises that the product will do something that benefits the consumer.
Example: A shampoo might promise to do away with split ends.
Student's Example

Sex Appeal: This technique attempts to convince consumers that using the product will make them more physically appealing to others.
Example: A skin lotion may claim to make skin soft enough to touch.
Student's Example

85

Statistical: This technique uses numbers to convince the consumer that this product is the best among its competition.
Example: A mouthwash company may announce that its product was chosen four times out of five in a survey of people 15–25 years old.
Student's Example

Testimonial: This technique uses individuals who state that the product worked for them. The implied message is that, if it worked for this person, it will work for you.
Example: A famous athlete proclaims her favorite toothpaste.
Student's Example

In the space below, write one sentence completing the following statement:
The new information I gained today about advertisements is:

Physical
Education

Playing Matball

Pam Eckhardt • Grades 6–8 Physical Education Teacher • Colorado Springs, CO

Student Objectives

Students will be able to:

- practice kicking, sprinting, and throwing skills.
- relate previous base-running strategies to a new game.
- increase levels of enjoyment of physical activity.

Materials Needed

Teacher:

- one 8–12" playground kickball
- four 8' x 4' tumbling mats

Students:

- "Playing Matball" rules sheet

Lesson Activity Process

Clock 45 minutes.

The teacher will:

1. Provide each student with a "Playing Matball" rules sheet. If a photocopy machine is not available, make a transparency of the rules sheet for an overhead projector. Review the worksheet verbally with students, and have volunteers lay out the base markers according to the diagram on the sheet.
2. Demonstrate, or have a student volunteer demonstrate, proper throwing and kicking techniques.
3. To determine whether students understand how to play the game, stand with students along the edge of the playing area, and have students answer these questions:
   - Where is the first-base mat? (The mat in the far right diagonal corner from the kicker)
   - How many bases does a runner successfully touch without being tagged to earn a run? (five bases—the first base must be touched twice)
   - Where is the kicking line behind which a kicker must stay when kicking the ball? (The designated kicking line)
   - Where does the kicking team stand while waiting to take their turn and kick? (Area against the wall to the right and behind the kicker)
   - How long can the pitcher hold the ball before

pitching? (10 seconds, or get a new pitcher)
   - In what ways can a runner be called out? (Any kicked ball caught in the air, even rebounds from the ceiling or walls; tagging a runner with a held or thrown ball; kicking a ball into foul territory)
3. Assign students to teams, and have one team member collect and return the rules sheets to you.
4. Begin play, officiate and monitor students' skills, and provide positive and corrective feedback on individual student execution of game skills. Encourage the use of strategy in kicking and throwing.
5. When the game is over, gather students in the center of the playing area. Ask if they have any questions about the game, suggestions for faster play or more active involvement, and whether they enjoyed matball.
   - Have a peer helper do the running after the student has kicked the ball; or, have the peer helper kick the ball and the student run the bases.
   - Make the court bigger or smaller to encourage successful play.
   - Use a Nerf ball.

Evaluation

Formal evaluation is not necessary for this game. The names of students who show individual improvement in kicking, throwing, or use of strategy could be noted. Individual and team use of strategy for placement of kicks and tagging of runners should increase during the class session, especially if this is the first time the game has been played by this class. Informative, incident-specific notes on class successes or problems should be sufficient for teacher revisions of the game for future use.

Tips for Success

- You may wish to start this activity with a discussion about sportsmanship and fair play.
- Adapt the playing area to the facility. A gymnasium is best. The game can be played outdoors and the distance between bases adjusted to the ability level of the students.

- Assigning teams should be quick. Possible methods of team assignment are:
  a. Alphabetical assignment (A through G, H through Z).
  b. Assignment by attendance squads.
  c. Assignment by date of birth (January through June and July through December; even- and odd-numbered months).
  d. Assignment by hair color, color of shirt, etc.
  e. Predetermined posted team lists established by the teacher or substitute.
- If unequal abilities exist among the teams, adjustments to the number or arrangement of players can be done by reassigning individuals or asking for volunteers to trade teams. Inequity of skill level adjustments should be done as soon as inequity is recognized—between innings, if possible, or a time-out can be called.
- To keep students active, students can kick and run in pairs. Both players run each time, but they alternate turns as the kicker. In this case, each player is considered an individual runner and each must be put out separately. If the kick is caught, only the player who kicked the ball is out—the other player can run to first and must be put out separately.
- Temporarily suspend play if rule clarification is needed or if the teacher can use the most current play to demonstrate the use of running or throwing strategies.
- You may wish to choose the pitcher yourself to avoid confusion or competition over which team member should pitch.

Additional Related Activities

1. Ask students to compare the rules of matball with rules of other ball games.
2. Have students brainstorm a new ball game. List suggested rules on the chalkboard. Then have students follow the rules they have created and play their new game.

87

Notes for Next Time

Playing Matball

Name _____   Date _____ Class _____

Object of Matball:

To kick the ball and run one circuit of the bases without being tagged by a thrown or held ball.

Rules

1. The pitcher must roll the ball directly to the kicker within 10 seconds of the time he or she receives the ball for each pitch.
2. Kickers must kick from behind the kicking line.
3. A kicker may refuse a pitch and roll the ball back to the pitcher. The second pitch must be kicked.
4. The runner must touch each base in the proper order. The runner must make a complete circuit of the bases to earn a run.
5. Runners must be on a base while the ball is in the pitcher's circle or on its way to the kicker. Once the ball is contacted by the kicker, the players may run to the next base.
6. Runners may advance any number of bases on a kick.
7. A runner is not required to run and may remain on any base for as long as he or she wishes. Runners may run on any out.
8. Any number of runners may occupy any base.
9. Every player kicks when it is his or her turn. The kicking order is the same for the entire game. The player next in line to kick at the end of an inning is the first to kick when the team returns to the kicking line.
10. A ball should not be caught in the air even if it rebounds off a wall or the ceiling. If the ball is caught before it hits the ground, the kicker is out.
11. Each team is allowed three outs per inning.
12. Bunting is not allowed.

Outs

1. Any kicked ball caught in the air, even a rebound from the walls or ceiling, is an out.
2. Any runner who is not on a base may be tagged with a held or thrown ball and is out.
3. A kicked ball must remain in the playing area until touched by a fielder or the kicker is out.

Playing Area

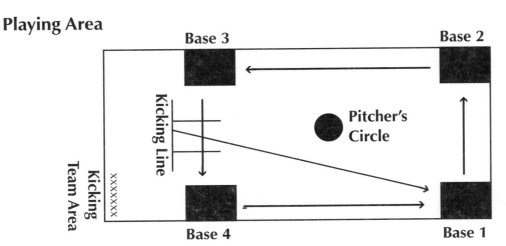

6-8

Art

Solving Problems Creatively

Polly Wolfe • Assistant Professor of Art Education • Muncie, IN

Student Objectives

Students will be able to:

- explore the creative problem-solving process by looking and thinking about abstract art works.
- exhibit fluency in generating many questions and answers about a work of art.
- exhibit consensus-building within their groups as they select a best question and answer concerning the work of art.
- evaluate the quality of their questions and answers.
- generate strategies for gaining more information about a work of art.

Materials Needed

Teacher:

- an abstract art reproduction for each small group (cubist, surrealist, impressionist, for example)
- kitchen timer

Students:

- "Solving Problems Creatively" worksheet
- pencil or pen
- paper

Lesson Activity Process

Clock 45-55 minutes.
The teacher will:

1. Divide students into groups of four or five, and give each group a different reproduction to study. Tell students that they won't actually be answering any questions today. Instead, they'll be thinking about how to answer a question.
2. Tell students that each of the steps of this lesson will be timed. Their job is to cooperate as a group, so they can do their best in a specific time frame.
3. After selecting a recorder for each group, set the kitchen timer for 6 minutes. Tell the groups to generate as many questions as possible regarding the work of art before the timer pings. All questions will be recorded by the recorder. NOTE: Even "silly" questions should be recorded.
4. Set the timer for 5 minutes. Instruct the groups to select the best (or most interesting) question from all

those generated and record that question on the chalkboard or on a transparency.

5. Set the timer for 6 minutes. During this time, the groups will generate the best answers to the selected question.
6. Set the timer for 6 minutes, during which groups will select the "best" (most plausible) answer to the selected question.
7. Set the timer for 10 minutes. Groups will have 8 minutes to create an action plan to find out more information about the work of art and an answer to the target question. Such resources as the art room, the art teacher, library resources like encyclopedias and biographies, and art books should be listed. In addition, assignments should be made for individual group members. At this time, getting answers to some of the other questions generated might be assigned as well.
8. During the remaining class time students individually complete the "Solving Problems Creatively" worksheet.

Modifications for Students with Special Needs

- Complete the lesson as a whole class, rather than in groups.
- Have the special needs student keep time.

Evaluation

After each activity, provide feedback to the students (based on teacher observations) to reinforce the desired group behavior. During class, note which groups are able to exhibit fluency in generating a large number of questions and answers on the recorders' sheets. Observe groups' consensus-building skills as they debate the "best question and answer" portion of the activity. The action plans of each group should reveal individual and group strategies for extending student knowledge about the artist and his or her works. The worksheet should reveal the extent of each student's involvement in the creative problem-solving process.

89

Answers to Student Worksheet

There are no "correct" answers to student worksheets. However, you may wish to make comments concerning the students' participation, what kind of questions and answers they generated, and the potential efficacy of their information-gathering strategies.

Tips for Success

- If you have difficulty obtaining several reproductions, you may choose to post one reproduction on the wall. All the groups can focus on one piece of art.
- The process that groups are to follow may be further explained by writing each step on the board or overhead (i.e., 1. List as many questions as you can about this work of art. 2. Select your best question, etc.).
- Ideally, groups should consist of no more than 6 and no less than 3 students. They may be best formed by proximity (for example, one group per table).
- Remind students that their job is to come up with questions, not to judge the questions others offer.
- Circulating to see how productive each group is may facilitate all students' involvement.
- Times indicated are only suggestions. Other parameters may be necessary to meet classroom or time **constrictions.**

Additional Related Activities

1. Review selected questions and answers of all groups in a whole class activity. Compare the questions and answers and what they deal with. How many deal with the form, the subject, or the meaning of the artwork?

2. As a class, review each group's action plan. Did different groups come up with different strategies or resources for finding more information? Would these strategies work when looking for information in other disciplines, like history or mathematics?

3. Have the groups follow their action plans and report their findings about the artist and his or her work to the class, either in an oral presentation or in written form.

Notes for Next Time

Solving Problems Creatively

Name _____ **Date** _____ **Class** _____

Title of Artwork

Artist

1. I generated _____ questions on the list in my group.

2. The best question I came up with was

3. I think the most interesting question asked was

4. My group thought the best question was

5. I do/don't agree with my group because

6. I think the best answer to the group's question is

7. My group thought that the best answer to the question was

8. My responsibility in finding out more information about _____ is

9. I will carry out my responsibility by following these steps:
   a.
   b.
   c.

10. I expect to find out that

91

Building Strong Communication Skills

Nancy Day • K–6 Guidance Counselor • Springfield, OH

Home Economics

Student Objectives

Students will be able to:

- practice both verbal and nonverbal communication skills.
- acquire active listening skills.
- create strategies to relate to others verbally and nonverbally.

Materials Needed

Teacher:

- about 20 pictures of simple objects (e.g., from a primary coloring book)

Students:

- "Building Strong Communication Skills" worksheet
- sheet of paper
- pencil

92

New Terminology

effective communication: when the active listener interprets the messenger's information in the same way that the sender intended it

nonverbal communication: communication without the use of words

messenger: the person sending the information

active listener: the person receiving the information

Lesson Activity Process

Clock 45–55 minutes.

The teacher will:

1. Discuss with students the meaning of effective communication and the concepts involved by explaining the new vocabulary. Indicate that the lesson today is practicing the art of effective communication.

2. Break the class into two equal groups. Without saying a word to each other, the students must nonverbally line up from the shortest to the tallest in their group. Have each group decide if the other was successful.

3. With the class still in two equal groups, tell students that, using nonverbal communication skills, group members are to line up according to their birthdays, from 1 January to 31 December.

4. Divide students into pairs, and have each student pair place two chairs back-to-back, spaced randomly about the room.

5. Within each pair, one student is the "messenger" and the other is the "active listener." Review each student's job. The messenger is given a picture. Using directions only, the messenger tries to tell the active listener how to draw the picture. The messenger must not, through his or her words, give away the picture's representation. So, for example, if it is a picture of a hat, the messenger may not say, "Draw a hat." Instead, the messenger's directions might start with, "On the right side of your paper, starting at about the middle of the page, draw a vertical line about as long as your finger." The listener is permitted to ask as many questions as necessary to reconstruct the picture, but the listener is not permitted to see the picture.

6. When the active listener feels that he or she has finished reconstructing the picture, the messenger can show the listener the true picture. Then students can start work on the "Building Strong Communication" worksheet.

Modifications for Students with Special Needs

- Allow the student to time the groups as they arrange themselves according to height and birthdays.
- Create simple shapes, such as a square or a triangle, for the student to describe.

Evaluation

Observation of student participation in both group and pair activities will serve for purposes of evaluation. Answers to the worksheet are neither right nor wrong, but depend instead on each student's experience during class. However, whether students complete their portions of the worksheet can be included in the evaluation.

Answers to Student Handout

Answers will vary.

Tips for Success

- If a copy machine is unavailable, you can draw your own forms for students to use in their pair activities. In addition, the questions on the worksheet can be written on the chalkboard.
- If there is an odd number of students, pair yourself with the unpaired student. You should act as active listener.
- The messenger should be encouraged to guard the picture, so the active listener isn't able to see it.
- Every "messenger" believes he or she is giving good instructions. The listeners find, however, that they rarely are able to duplicate the pictures. They do find this activity enjoyable, and discussing student responses to the end-of-activity worksheet is enlightening for all.

Notes for Next Time

Additional Related Activities

1. If time permits, have student pairs switch pictures and roles—the messenger becomes the active listener, and the active listener becomes the messenger. Students then can complete the other half of their worksheets.
2. Have students sit in a large circle around the room and play the "Gossip Game." Whisper a message to the first student in the circle; that student whispers to the next, and so on. (The message could be something like, "Mrs. Brown's black cow disappeared last night.") Have the final student tell the message that he or she heard and compare it to the message you sent. Ask students, What does this tell students about communicating?

Building Strong Communication Skills

Name _____   Date _____ Class _____

For the Messenger

1. As the "messenger," what made this picture difficult to explain to your partner?

2. Did you feel that you were giving instructions well?

3. What would have made this picture easier to draw?

For the Active Listener

1. As an "active listener," what made this picture difficult to draw?

2. Did you feel you were following instructions correctly?

3. What would have made this picture easier to draw?

Conducting a Survey

Helen Follis • Grade 5 Teacher • Tallahassee, FL

Critical Thinking

Student Objectives

Students will be able to:

*   select an appropriate topic to survey.
*   design a question related to that topic.
*   survey the target audience.
*   analyze the results of the survey.
*   utilize higher-level thinking skills of application, analysis, synthesis, and evaluation.

Materials Needed

Teacher:

*   chalkboard or overhead projector

Students:

*   pencil
*   paper
*   copy of "Conducting a Survey" worksheet
*   calculator (optional)

New Terminology

survey: to ask people a question in order to collect data for analysis

opinion: belief

preference: liking something better than another

tally: a recorded account

percent: one part in a hundred

Lesson Activity Process

Clock 45–55 minutes.

The teacher will:

1. Ask students, "What is the most popular pizza topping?" Once the din clears, tell them you have a way to answer that question by conducting a survey.

2. First, write the question on the board, then ask students to brainstorm possibilities. List the possibilities in a column under the question. Next, ask for a show of hands to indicate students' preferences. Tally the results next to each topping. The completed list might look something like this:

    sausage 7
    pepperoni 15
    cheese 4
    mushroom 3
    everything 5

Share with students that the numbers in their tally indicate the topping considered most popular by the class—which is most popular?

3. Tell students, "Now we want to analyze our results in terms of percent." There is an easy way to tell the percent of people who preferred the most popular. Find the total number of people who answered the question, (in the example of above, the number of students is 34), and put that on the bottom of a fraction (the denominator). Now put the number of people preferring the favorite (in example, pepperoni, 15) on top of the fraction (the numerator). The fraction is 15/34. Use a calculator to figure 15 divided by 34 equals 44 percent.

4. Continue this process with each number generated by the survey, listing first the fraction, then the percentage, next to the number indicated for each topping.

5. Distribute copies of the "Conducting a Survey" worksheet, and direct students to conduct their own surveys. Help them determine a suitable question. Give examples that would lend themselves to a survey: favorite musical group or soloist, favorite school subjects, favorite recent movie, favorite sports or teams, favorite hobbies, etc. Discourage yes/no questions or questions that would cause each student to respond with a different answer. The best questions are those that yield clusters of responses on each possible answer.

6. Tell students that they must survey 15 students in the class and write their responses on the worksheet. Explain that they have 10 minutes in which to conduct their surveys.

7. When the 10 minutes are up, call the group members back together and have them tally their responses using the bottom of their handouts. Direct them to show each tally as a fraction, then to use a calculator to show the fraction as a percent.

8. Have each student read his or her question to the class and identify the most popular response.

Modifications for Students with Special Needs

- Have a peer helper do the writing for the student.
- Have other students come to the student's desk to offer their responses to the survey.
- Help the student construct his or her questions.

Evaluation

An initial evaluation should be conducted to determine the suitability of the questions students have selected for their surveys. Accuracy of students' completed worksheets also can be evaluated.

Answers to Student Handout

Answers will vary depending on the survey topic and student responses.

Tips for Success

- To check students' understanding of fractions and percents, use a simple assessment such as, "Use a calculator to write these fractions as percents: 1/4, 1/5, 2/3, 4/7, and 7/16." This review can be taught before students attempt to analyze survey results.
- If calculators are not available, have volunteers work the percents manually on the chalkboard.
- Because this lesson involves students in both critical thinking and number operations, you may need to model planning and decision making for students. Before they begin the assignment, "think out loud" about the steps involved in selecting a topic to survey, as well as the recordkeeping that must be done in conjunction with the survey.

Notes for Next Time

Additional Related Activities

1. Conclude the analysis by constructing a circle graph to illustrate the percentage of preferences indicated by the survey on pizza toppings. Use given percents to calculate "the biggest piece of pie" in the circle graph. Rather than involving students in complicated calculations to determine the exact slice of the circle graph indicated by a response, they can estimate the sizes of sections "Draw a line to divide your circle in half. What percent is represented by each half? (50 percent) Now, divide each half into half. What fraction does each half of a half represent? (1/4) What percent? (25 percent) Now divide each quarter in half. What fraction does this represent? (1/8) What percent? (12.5 percent) Divide one more time. What fraction? (1/16) What percent? (6.25 percent) "We can use these figures to help us find the right sized piece of pie for our own circle graphs. The pepperoni section of our graph needs to show 44 percent. I can make 44 percent like this: 1/4, or 25 percent, plus 1/8, or 12.5 percent, plus 1/16 or 6.25 percent. How much do I still need to make 44 percent? (HINT: add 25 + 12.5 + 6.25.) I still need 0.25 percent, or just a tiny piece more. Now, I will shade in 1/4 (25 percent), 1/8 (12.5 percent), 1/16 (6.25 percent) and just a tiny piece more to show the 44 percent of the class that prefers pepperoni." Repeat this procedure for each graph section.

2. Have students use what they have learned to construct their own circle graphs to illustrate their survey results.

3. Have students think about how conducting an interview would be different from conducting a survey. Explain that some of the same critical thinking processes are used in planning, decision making, analysis, application, synthesis, and evaluation.

96

Conducting a Survey

Name _____ Date _____ Class _____

Question _____

**Record each student's response to his or her number,
tally responses by category, then figure percentages.**

1. _____   15. _____
2. _____   16. _____
3. _____   17. _____
4. _____   18. _____
5. _____   19. _____
6. _____   20. _____
7. _____   21. _____
8. _____   22. _____
9. _____   23. _____
10. _____   24. _____
11. _____   25. _____
12. _____   26. _____
13. _____   27. _____
14. _____   28. _____

Category 1 _____ Tally _____ Fraction _____ Percent _____

Category 2 _____ Tally _____ Fraction _____ Percent _____

Category 3 _____ Tally _____ Fraction _____ Percent _____

Category 4 _____ Tally _____ Fraction _____ Percent _____

Category 5 _____ Tally _____ Fraction _____ Percent _____

Category 6 _____ Tally _____ Fraction _____ Percent _____

Chapter 7

High School Lesson Activities

What Is a High School Like?

Today's high schools are big, busy places consisting of grades 9–12 or 10–12. There are usually more students, teachers, administrators, and support staff—including security—on high school campuses than on elementary and middle school campuses. High schools are generally organized departmentally because the teachers have been trained as subject area specialists; however, a current trend is to integrate the secondary school curriculum more fully. Most high schools operate on a six-, seven-, or eight-period schedule with 40–55 minutes for each class period. Throughout the day students move from class to class, with 3–5 minutes between classes. A variety of individual schedules exist—some seniors may have only a half-day of classes, some students may attend special off-campus programs, or some students may eat lunch before fourth period while others eat after fourth period.

Most high schools have rich extracurricular programs consisting of team and individual sports, service and academic clubs, debate and drama teams, and newspaper and yearbook groups. Secondary schools prepare students to enter advanced programs of study or to enter the job market upon graduation. Some high schools track students according to ability—with different levels of classes in each of the core subject areas. Other high schools (especially in urban areas) are magnet schools, which gear instruction to students with special interests such as the performing arts or mathematics and science.

What Are High School Students Like?

Adults frequently have a negative perception of adolescents due to the negative image of them often presented in the media. Teachers of adolescents should focus upon these students' positive qualities and should possess an understanding of their unique needs and characteristics. High school students are active, enthusiastic, energetic, humorous, straightforward, serious, and talkative. As they seek independence from adults, adolescents turn to peers, who greatly influence their behavior—including speech, dress, and interests. Being popular and part of the "in group" become important at this time. School is more often seen as a place to socialize than as a place to acquire knowledge. Talking and interacting with each other consumes a great deal of adolescents' time. Although being accepted by peers is very important, adolescents are also striving to create a separate, unique identity. A normal part of this identity-seeking process is trying new behaviors and attitudes, which partially explains the unpredictable nature of high school students.

As a result of the challenges in society today, high school students often face difficulties with drugs and alcohol, sexually transmitted disease and pregnancy, gang membership, suicide, and separated families. Teachers must be sensitive to these pressures that adolescents encounter and be willing to empathize and act as an advocate for students. Validating their concerns and giving them opportunities to talk are ways high school teachers can meet the needs of adolescents. Some adolescents turn from parents and family to teachers as role models.

Changes in mental processes occur during adolescence. Students move from being able to think concretely to being able to think abstractly. Because of this change in thinking abilities, they are able to imagine possibilities and find "what if" questions stimulating. Such newfound mental capabilities help to account for adolescents' preoccupation with daydreaming. Teachers should tap adolescents' imaginations and encourage creativity through questions and assignments they plan. Because of their increased ability to think logically, high school students can set goals and systemati-cally plan how to achieve the outcomes. Focusing their thoughts upon the future occupies much of adolescents' time. As they question traditional values and positions, adolescents find writing down their thoughts and reflections to be a meaningful activity. Even though peers are important to adolescents so is spending time alone. Parents and teachers must demonstrate respect for this need.

What Responsibilities Might You Have?

High school students may seem overly critical of their teachers. However, they do hold high expectations, and substitutes are not exempt from these expectations. They want to be taught by someone who is competent in working with adolescents and in communicating the subject matter. While these students realize that substitute teaching is a difficult job, they expect quality instruction—not mere "babysitting." If you are substituting outside your area of expertise, it is acceptable to admit that you do not have all the answers. Students will appreciate your honesty.

Responsibilities of substitute teachers might include hall duty (monitoring student behavior before school, between classes, and at lunch), conducting restroom checks, accompanying students on a field trip, collecting forms and money, making school announcements, checking attendance, and teaching classes. Effective substitutes are essential partners in the successful operation of the high school. It is important to be aware of procedures as well as special programs and events. The department chair and/or the school principal—along with the school handbook—are your best sources of information. Helping adolescents make the transition into the adult world is very rewarding work. Watching students become more responsible allows you to share in this important task. As a substitute teacher, you can model the value of being flexible and adaptable as you meet the challenges of teaching.

The lesson plans in this section offer ideas for delivering content in different subject areas. Keep in mind that students want to be engaged in constructive activities that allow them to interact with one another. Also take note that the best preventive discipline strategy is a

99

well-planned lesson. Here are a few tips to guide your effort in the classroom:

1. State your expectations clearly and in a firm manner. Students cannot read your mind and are more likely to test you if your expectations are unstated.

2. Encourage students to participate and provide opportunities to do so. Ask for student input, allow students to write on the chalkboard, and engage them in discussions. The more actively involved students are in the classroom, the more on-task they will remain.

3. Begin and end class on time. By starting as soon as the bell rings, you communicate that what you have planned is important. You also respect their need to go to another class by finishing when the bell rings.

4. Hold students accountable by collecting work at the end of the period. Students need to know that the work they have produced is valued.

5. Find ways to let students talk to each other about the subject matter. Working with a partner is often a useful technique.

6. Make sure the pace of the lesson does not drag. Look for nonverbal signs that this is happening. When the pace is too slow (or too fast), students are likely to get off-task and their attention is hard to regain.

7. Model good manners by saying "please," "thank you," "I appreciate," and by not talking while someone else is and not raising your voice in anger. Sometimes speaking softly is more effective than shouting loudly.

100

Writing Clear Directions

Terrie St. Michel • High School English Teacher • Phoenix, AZ

Student Objectives

Students will be able to:

- write directions.
- follow directions.
- write with specificity and accuracy.
- interact in small groups.
- reproduce a specific design.

Materials Needed

Students:

- pen or pencil
- paper

Lesson Activity Process

Clock 45 minutes.

The teacher will:

1. Tell each student to draw a simple design of his or her own choice. This design is to be kept private and confidential. NOTE: The point of this assignment is for students to write accurate directions for reproducing the design; therefore, the original design must be kept secret.

2. Now tell each student to write clear and accurate directions for reproducing his or her design.

3. Students will then select partners. One student will be "Partner A" and the other, "Partner B."

4. Have Partner A give the written directions for his or her secret design to Partner B. Partner B is to draw the secret design based on these written directions.

5. At the same time, Partner B is to give his or her set of written directions to Partner A. Partner A is to draw partner B's secret design based on these directions.

6. Allow students 5–7 minutes to create their drawings. Then have them check their work against the original drawings.

7. Next, if the drawings do not match, ask the partner pairs to discuss what is missing or inaccurate in the written directions. Also, have students comment about the relationship between the original design, the written directions, and the subsequent response drawing (positive or negative, what worked, what didn't work, etc.).

8. Have students share their partner's designs and discuss the accuracy of the directions and the specifics needed to make more detailed designs.

9. Ask students to repeat the entire exercise with a different partner, creating new designs and writing new directions.

Modifications for Students with Special Needs

- Provide a visual example before assigning students their tasks.
- Allow additional time, if necessary.
- Have pairs consist of one student with and one student without special needs.

Evaluation

Evaluations should be made on students' second set of directions and drawings, to allow students to learn from their first drawing-directions set. Students should identify any confusing parts of the directions. Criteria should be the accuracy of the drawing.

Tips for Success

- Lead a discussion about the language clues (e.g., vertical, horizontal, perpendicular, etc.) that are necessary for the written directions in this assignment.
- You may wish to pair students alphabetically or with their next-door-neighbor. If the class has an odd number of students, create one group of three.
- Circulate among the students while they are drawing and discussing with their partners, and offer suggestions.
- Ask students with especially well-written directions to read them to the class.

101

Additional Related Activities

1. Provide students with other sets of directions—examples are directions from a cookbook, for experiments in their science books, from an automobile manual, or in a computer book. Read the directions aloud, then ask students to discuss whether the directions are well-written or ambiguous. When they have identified a set of directions that they consider well-written, ask students to identify the key words or phrases that make the directions easy for people to follow.

2. Draw a simple design on the chalkboard, and have each student write drawing directions for the design. Then compare the directions by reading selected (anonymous) sets out loud. Ask students to determine the best-written directions for that design.

Notes for Next Time

9–12 Creating a Character
Composition

Lori D'Achino Bucco • Grade 11 English Teacher • Falls Church, VA

Student Objectives

Students will be able to:

- discuss the ideas of character and personality as they apply to a character in a piece of fiction.
- look to detail in their writing.
- develop a fictional character completely.

Materials Needed

Students:

- pen or pencil
- paper
- "Creating a Character" worksheet

Lesson Activity Process

Clock 45–55 minutes.

The teacher will:

1. Ask students to name their favorite fictional characters. Have students tell what they know about each fictional character identified.
2. Distribute copies of the worksheet. Tell students that they will create their own fictional characters by completing the worksheet. Remind students to add at least three additional categories and answer them for their characters.
3. After the worksheets are complete, read the following scenario aloud to the class:
   Your character is walking through a park near his or her home. Suddenly, the character comes across a lost and crying six-year-old. How does your character respond? What is your character thinking? What is the conversation between your character and the child? How is the situation resolved? How does your character feel about what happened after it is all over?
4. Tell each student to write a descriptive piece of fiction (approximately 250 words in length) about the way the character that he or she has developed would react in the situation you just described.
5. When students have completed their writing assignment, lead a discussion in which students describe their fictional characters and explain the characters' reactions. Ask whether any particular category on the worksheet helped students determine how the **characters would react.**

Modifications for Students with Special Needs

- Provide several photographs as guidelines as the student develops the character.
- Allow the student to relate the character's reactions orally rather than in writing.
- Assign a peer helper.

Evaluation

Base your evaluation on whether the student completed the worksheet without discrepancies in the character being described, and on whether the reaction to the scenario seems appropriate for the created character. Class discussion also can be used for evaluation purposes.

Answers to Student Handout

Answers will vary entirely based upon the character the student has created.

Tips for Success

- As students begin completing their worksheets, caution them to read through the whole worksheet before beginning to answer. Also, remind students to check that no answer contradicts the previous answers.
- Ask students what additional categories would have helped them describe their character's reaction to the above scenario. Possible additional categories include favorite color, film, actor, food, song, sport, clothing style, season, novel, television show; name of high school; and kind of neighborhood.
- When evaluating this activity, you may wish to ignore misspellings and errors in grammar and punctuation in student writing. It is the depth of each character's development that will measure success or failure of the activity.
- Tell students that, as they write, they may go back to their worksheets and make changes, if necessary.
- You also can participate in the lesson activity, and allow your fact sheet and prose to withstand the same scrutiny as the work of the students.

103

Additional Related Activities

1. Have the students fill out a fact sheet on the six-year-old child in the scenario to which the students have responded. Ask the students for as much detail about the child as they have provided about the character of their own invention. This is a particularly successful assignment for students who liked the worksheet better than the prose writing.

2. Present a different scenario to the students in which their characters can take part (for example, surviving a plane crash, witnessing a robbery, or finding a wallet full of money).

3. Ask the students to develop their own scenarios and to include their own characters.

4. Have students leaf through magazines looking for a photograph of someone who reminds them of the character they created. (If they wish, students can choose to draw a representation of their character instead.) Then attach the photos and drawings to the worksheets and put them on display around the room.

Notes for Next Time

Creating a Character

Name _____ **Date** _____ **Class** _____

Read the entire worksheet before you begin to answer the questions in order to avoid potential conflicts in your answers. Fill out the following fact sheet with as much detail as possible. If your character is young, use your discretion about filling in answers. For example, if your character is 12, you may not be able even to project an answer about a spouse, but if he is 20, you may talk about a girlfriend. Sometimes you will write down dates that have passed, like birth dates, and for others you may write down future dates, like the projected graduation date of a 12-year-old.

Character Fact Sheet

Character's full name
Gender
Age
Birth date
Astrological sign
Weight
Hair color
Eye color
Scars or identifying marks
Complexion
Glasses or contact lenses
Braces
Any disabilities
Father's name
Mother's name
Birth order
Number of siblings (names and ages)
Character's favorite sibling
Religious affiliation
Marital status
Spouse
Wedding date
Any children (names and ages)
Pets
Job
Hobbies
Hometown

List at least three additional categories and answer them for your character.

105

Correcting Algebra Errors

Hazel H. Orth • High School Mathematics Teacher • McLean, VA

Student Objectives

Students will be able to:

- scan an algebra paper for errors in symbols and syntax.
- analyze the errors encountered and correct the errors.
- describe the problem and the mathematical rules used to simplify or solve that problem to other members of their group.

Materials Needed

Students:

- pencil
- "Correcting Algebra Errors" worksheet
- algebra text (optional)

Lesson Activity Process

Clock 45–55 minutes.

The teacher will:

1. Divide the class into groups of 3–4 students. This may be accomplished by counting off or the class may already have cooperative learning groups. Assign each group a number to facilitate the evaluation process.

2. Write the following algebra problem on the chalkboard:

$$4x - 13 = 7x + 14$$
$$4x - 4x - 13 = 7x - 4x + 14$$
$$-13 = 3x + 14$$
$$-13 + 14 = 3x$$
$$1 = 3x$$
$$1/3 = x$$

3. Tell the groups that something is wrong with the problem. Instruct each group to identify both the error and the mathematical rule that has not been followed in the example. NOTE: Students may need to refer to their textbooks to use the correct mathematical terminology in describing both the error and the rule.

4. After three or four minutes of group discussion, ask one group to send a representative to the chalkboard to circle the problem and write the correct rule. Students in other groups may ask questions of the representative about the problem and may ask you questions about the exercise. [-13 -14 = 3x; x = -9]

5. Distribute the "Correcting Algebra Errors" worksheets.

6. Tell the groups that members may complete the worksheet together, although each student should fill in his or her own worksheet. In addition, have group members check each other's work. Tell students they have 30 minutes for this assignment.

7. When the groups have completed their worksheets, lead a discussion in which students talk about which is more difficult—finding the error or simply solving the problem. Also ask students to tell which problems were easiest and which were most difficult.

Modifications for Students with Special Needs

- Pair student with peer helper and allow them to complete the worksheet together.
- Work each problem on the chalkboard, as a class, instead of completing the worksheets in small groups.

Evaluation

The groups' work habits can be evaluated for listening, keeping "on task," etc., by using the cooperative learning checklist on page 112. During the lesson, students should demonstrate their group processing skills, critical thinking and reading skills, knowledge of the rules of mathematics, and awareness of their skill development as a learner.

Answers to Student Worksheet

[see replication of student worksheet with answers marked on pages 110–11]

1. This does not use the order of operations.
2. The operation sign was omitted.
3. The odd exponent keeps the negative sign.
4. Exponents indicate the number of factors of the binomial.
5. The words "less than" indicate the 4 is being subtracted.
6. The prepositional phrase (of a number and four) indicates parentheses.
7. John's age is in terms of Kerry's age.
8. For power to a power, exponents are multiplied.
9. The base for the 5th power is only the x.
10. The negative is distributed to each term.

Tips for Success
- Tell students they are allowed to use calculators, if available.
- As students work on their assignments, circulate around the room, encouraging groups to discuss their decisions and the wording of their answers.
- If students identify problems they have yet to study, ask them to try the problems anyway and do the best they can. Explain that the problems will not be counted against them.

Additional Related Activities
1. Have students use the mathematical formulas they most recently studied to make up a five-question quiz. Tell students to make an error purposefully in each formula. Then have students exchange their papers and find the errors.

Notes for Next Time

2. Direct students to write a short analysis of the skills used in this lesson and how mastery of these skills might help the students perform better on tests and quizzes.
3. Have students discuss the process of the lesson in a whole class setting. Point out that eliminating errors is essential in the real workplace, and groups are often held responsible for the project regardless of the work efforts of one individual. Ask questions like:
   - For what specific types of errors would you scan your test or quiz paper?
   - Which rules were ignored by the author?
   - Specify the types of mistakes you make most often.
   - How could you avoid those errors?
4. Have students solve the problems.

Find the Error

Name _____ Group _____

There is a single error in each problem. Identify the error by circling the step in which the error occurs. On the lines provided beneath the problem, write an explanation of the mathematical rule or rules that were not followed. Use complete sentences and correct mathematical terminology. You may only consult and share answers within your group.

Simplify each expression:

1. $\dfrac{2+48(5-3)}{9-7}$

    $\dfrac{50(5-3)}{9-7}$

    $\dfrac{50(2)}{2}$

    50

    _____

    _____

2. $16(13 - 8) - [40(5 - 4)] \div (10 - 5)$

    $16(5)(40 \div 5)$

    $16(5)(8)$

    640

    _____

    _____

Evaluate each expression if $x = 3$ and $y = -2$

3. $y^3 - x^2$

    $(-2)^3 - (3)^2$

    $8 - 9$

    -1

    _____

    _____

4. $(x - y)^3$

    $(3^3 + 2^3)$

    $(27 + 8)$

    35

    _____

    _____

Translate each phrase from words into algebraic symbols. Let n = the number.

5. Four less than twice a number, n _____ $4 - 2n$ _____

_____

_____

_____

6. Three times the sum of a number, n, and four _____ $3n + 4$ _____

_____

_____

_____

Find the Error

7. If Kerry is x years old today and John is 5 years older, how old was John 7 years ago?

$$x - 7 \underline{\hspace{3cm}}$$

_____

Simplify each expression

8. $(2x^3)^4$
   2^4x^7
   $16x^7$

   _____

   _____

   _____

9. $(2x^5)(5^2x^4)$
   $32x^5(25x^4)$
   $800x^9$

   _____

   _____

   _____

10. $(3m^3 - 5m^2 + 7) - (4m^3 + 6m^2 - 3)$
    $3m^3 - 5m^2 + 7 - 4m^3 - 6m^2 - 3$
    $-m^3 - 11m^2 + 4$

    _____

    _____

    _____

Discussion

What skills did you need to use in your group or by yourself in order to eliminate the errors in this worksheet?

Find the Error

Name _Key_ _____ **Group** _____

There is a single error in each problem. Identify the error by circling the step in which the error occurs. On the lines provided beneath the problem, write an explanation of the mathematical rule or rules that were not followed. Use complete sentences and correct mathematical terminology. You may only consult and share answers within your group.

Simplify each expression:

1. $\dfrac{2+48(5-3)}{9-7}$ $\dfrac{2+48(2)}{2}$

   $\dfrac{50(5-3)}{9-7}$ $\dfrac{2+96}{2}$

   $\dfrac{50(2)}{2}$ $98/2=49$

   50

   This does not use the order of operations.

2. $16(13-8)-[40(5-4)]\div(10-5)$ $16(5)-\cancel{(40)}$
   $16(5)(40\div5)$ $80-8$
   $16(5)(8)$ 72
   640

   The operation sign was omitted.

110

Evaluate each expression if $x=3$ and $y=-2$
3. y^3-x^2
   $(-2)^3-(3)^2$
   $8-9$ $-8-9$
   -1 -17

   The odd exponent keeps the negative sign.

4. $(x-y)^3$ $($
   (3^3+2^3) 5
   $(27+8)$ 125
   35

   Exponents indicate the number of factors of
   the binomial

Translate each phrase from words into algebraic symbols. Let n = the number.

5. Four less than twice a number, n _____ $4-2n$ $2n-4$

   The words "less than" indicate the 4 is being subtracted.

6. Three times the sum of a number, n, and four _____ $3n+4$ $3(n+4)$

   The prepositional phrase (of a number and four) indicates parentheses.

Find the Error

Name _Key_   **Date** _____ **Class** _____

7. If Kerry is x years old today and John is 5 years older, how old was John 7 years ago?

$$x - 7 \quad \underline{x+5-7 \ \text{or} \ x-2}$$

John's age is in terms of Kerry's age. _____

Simplify each expression

8. $(2x^3)^4$

    2^4x^7 $2 \times$

    $16x^7$ 1

_____

For   _exponents_

multipled

9. $(2x^5)(5^2x^4)$

    $32x^5(25x^4)$ $2 \ \bullet$

    $800x^9$ 5

_____

The base for the 5th power is only the x.   _power_

_____

10. $(3m^3 - 5m^2 + 7) - (4m^3 + 6m^2 - 3)$

    $3m^3 - 5m^2 + 7 - 4m^3 - 6m^2 - 3$ $3m^3 - 5m^2 + 7 - 4m^3 - 6m^2 + 3$

    $-m^3 - 11m^2 + 4$ $- - \quad +$

_____

The negative is distributed to each term.

_____

Discussion

What skills did you need to use in your group or by yourself in order to eliminate the errors in this worksheet?

Cooperation Learning Group

Use this as a simple checklist to evaluate group processing during an activity. Record each skill as it is demonstrated by each group.

Group 1
___ listening
___ on task
___ questioning
___ using correct terminology
___ courtesy
___ decision making

Group 2
___ listening
___ on task
___ questioning
___ using correct terminology
___ courtesy
___ decision making

Group 3
___ listening
___ on task
___ questioning
___ using correct terminology
___ courtesy
___ decision making

Group 4
___ listening
___ on task
___ questioning
___ using correct terminology
___ courtesy
___ decision making

Group 5
___ listening
___ on task
___ questioning
___ using correct terminology
___ courtesy
___ decision making

Group 6
___ listening
___ on task
___ questioning
___ using correct terminology
___ courtesy
___ decision making

Group 7
___ listening
___ on task
___ questioning
___ using correct terminology
___ courtesy
___ decision making

Group 8
___ listening
___ on task
___ questioning
___ using correct terminology
___ courtesy
___ decision making

Group 9
___ listening
___ on task
___ questioning
___ using correct terminology
___ courtesy
___ decision making

Building Molecules

Joan E. Vallee • Assistant Professor of Chemistry • Lake Charles, LA

Student Objectives

Students will be able to:

*   visualize the orientation of atoms in molecules through three-dimensional models.
*   construct models of simple molecules using gumdrops and toothpicks.
*   discern the effect of outer level electrons on the shapes and polarities of molecules.
*   predict shapes and polarities of other molecules based on these models.

Materials Needed

Teacher:

*   one bag of small and one bag of large gumdrops
*   toothpicks

Students:

*   copy of "Building Molecules" worksheet
*   pencil

New Terminology

modified Lewis structure: a representation of an atom's valence (outer shell) electrons, which shows how electrons are distributed around the atom. Small dots represent lone electron pairs (unshared), and dashes represent shared electrons (one electron contributed by each atom to form the covalent bond)

molecular geometry: the three-dimensional arrangement of atoms around a central atom

nonpolar molecule: one having symmetrical charge distribution

polar molecule: one having unequal charge distribution

Lesson Activity Process

Clock 45–55 minutes.

The teacher will:

1. Lead a discussion in which students volunteer everything they remember about atoms and molecules. Students should indicate that an atom is a basic unit of matter, with a nucleus surrounded by one or more "orbiting" electrons. Some of these electrons are paired up (lone electron pairs). Some of these electrons are shared with other atoms, forming a covalent bond that creates a molecule. Molecules are made up of atoms whose covalent bonds hold the atoms together in certain arrangements.
    Explain to students that some molecules are arranged symmetrically—that is, the atoms in the molecule are equally distributed and are called nonpolar molecules. Other molecules have unequally distributed atoms and are called polar molecules.
2. Divide the class into teams of two or three members. Distribute to each team 12–15 small gumdrops, several large gumdrops, a dozen toothpicks, and the "Building Molecules" worksheet.
3. Tell each group to choose one two-atom molecule, one three-atom molecule, one four-atom molecule, and one five-atom molecule from the worksheet. Their assignment is to use the gumdrops and toothpicks to construct their chosen molecules. Explain that students should follow the rules listed on the handout.
4. Have the groups share their completed molecules with the class, asking the class to identify each molecule by its gumdrop structure.
5. Finally, as a class, let the students determine the shapes possible for different numbers of atoms in a molecule. (In general, they will decide that two atoms sharing electrons can only be linear. Three atoms can be linear or bent. Four atoms can be trigonal planar or trigonal pyramidal. Five atoms will usually be tetrahedral.)

Modifications for Students with Special Needs

*   Assign a peer helper for group activity.
*   Follow the steps above as a class, rather than in groups.

Evaluation

Assess the comprehension of students by observing them as they first construct, then defend, their molecular models as teams. For individual assessment and to determine where further assistance is needed, correct the worksheets.

113

Answers to Student Worksheet

I. A. 1. one bond, no lone pairs
            linear
            nonpolar
        2. one bond, 6 lone pairs
            linear
            nonpolar
            (3 lone pairs on each chlorine)
        3. one bond, 3 lone pairs on Cl
            linear
            polar

    B. 1. two bonds, 2 lone pairs on O
            bent
            polar
        2. four bonds, 4 lone pairs
            linear
            nonpolar
            (2 lone pairs on each oxygen)
        3. two bonds, 6 lone pairs
            linear
            nonpolar

    C. 1. three bonds, 9 lone pairs
            trigonal planar
            nonpolar
        2. three bonds, 1 lone pair on N
            trigonal pyramidal
            polar

    D. 1. four bonds, no lone pairs
            tetrahedral
            nonpolar
        2. four bonds, 3 lone pairs on Cl
            tetrahedral
            polar
        3. four bonds, 9 lone pairs on Cl
            tetrahedral
            polar

II.
        1. shape of ammonia (P)
        2. shape of carbon dioxide (NP)
        3. shape of chlorine (NP)
        4. shape of chloromethane (P)
        5. shape of boron trifluoride (NP)
        6. shape of hydrogen chloride (P)

114

Tips for Success

*   Review basic concepts of polar and nonpolar bonds. Remind students that atoms are "in competition" for shared electrons in a covalent bond. Explain the difference between shared electrons in a covalent bond and unshared electrons, which occur as a lone pair. Refer to the Lewis structures of hydrogen, chlorine, and hydrogen chloride. The diatomic elements of hydrogen and chlorine would have nonpolar bonds but are also nonpolar diatomic molecules. The molecule hydrogen chloride has a polar bond but is also a polar molecule. Stress the fact that larger molecules may be nonpolar in symmetry but contain polar bonds.
*   During this activity, rotate among the teams to ensure that all students have an understanding of the rules.
*   Teams should be encouraged to work independently.
*   Following the guideline that the most stable structure is the one in which the electron pairs (toothpicks) are as far apart as possible will result in the best model of each molecule.
*   Displaying plastic models (borrowed from a math teacher) would help to show the various molecular shapes of simple molecules. When the activity is completed, these can be compared with the gumdrop models.
*   Students love this activity because it is one of the few they get to eat when they complete it. Building molecules provides them with a way to visualize the rather abstract concept of molecular geometry and allows them to predict shapes and polarities.

Additional Related Activities

1. If you are still in the classroom on test day, hang large gumdrop molecules across the front of the room and ask students to propose possible molecules based on the numbers and colors of gumdrops and the distribution of toothpicks (representing bonds and lone electron pairs).

2. Students can determine bond angles between the different bonds in their molecular models. A molecule with a linear shape would have a bond angle of 180 degrees. A molecule that is trigonal planar would have bond angles of both 120 degrees and 180

degrees. Bent, trigonal pyramidal, and tetrahedral molecules each have bond angles of 109.5 degrees. These angles can best be seen in the molecular models the teams have constructed.

3. Another concept that can be introduced is that of high electron density. The number of regions of high electron density can also be used to help determine molecular shapes.

4. Students may want to investigate additional shapes for more complicated molecules such as square pyramidal, trigonal bipyramidal, seesaw, and octahedral. Just viewing these shapes would be fun for most students. Understanding how these geometries are predicted, however, would require a more advanced knowledge of molecular theory.

Notes for Next Time

Building Molecules

Name _____ Date _____ Class _____

Construct molecule models by following these directions, then answer the questions below.

1. Use same-color, same-size gumdrops to represent atoms of the same element; use different-color gumdrops to represent different elements in the same molecule.

2. Determine whether there is a central atom (an atom that occurs only once in the molecule), and use a large gumdrop to represent it. Small gumdrops will represent the other atoms.

3. Put a gumdrop on each end of a toothpick to represent a covalent bond. A lone electron pair should be represented by a toothpick with a gumdrop on only one end.

4. Place toothpicks (which represent electron pairs either as bonds or lone electron pairs) into the central gumdrop so that they are as far apart as possible.

5. Below, dotted lines indicate covalent bonds going away from you; wedge lines indicate covalent bonds coming out toward you.

Molecular Models

I. Determine the number of bonds and lone electron pairs for one molecule in each of the following sections (A, B, C, and D), and construct a gumdrop model that represents its geometry.

A. Molecules having two atoms

1. hydrogen (H_2)   H—H

2. chlorine (Cl_2)   :C̈l—C̈l:

3. hydrogen chloride (HCl)   H—C̈l:

B. Molecules having three atoms

1. water (H_2O)

2. carbon dioxide (CO_2)   :O=C=O:

3. beryllium chloride ($BeCl_2$)   :C̈l—Be—C̈l:

Building Molecules

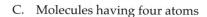

C. Molecules having four atoms

1. boron trifluoride (BF$_3$)

    ```
         :F:
          |
          B
       :F   F:
    ```

2. ammonia (NH$_3$)

    ```
        ..
        N....H
       /   \
      H     H
    ```

D. Molecules having five atoms

1. methane (CH$_4$)

    ```
         H
         |
         C....H
       /   \
      H     H
    ```

2. chloromethane (CH$_3$Cl)

    ```
        :Cl:
          |
          C....H
       /   \
      H     H
    ```

3. chloroform (CHCl$_3$)

    ```
         H
         |
         C....Cl:
       /   \
     :Cl   Cl:
    ```

II. Based on the shapes and polarities of the above molecules, predict the shape and polarity of each of the molecules below.

1. PH$_3$

    ```
        ..
        P....H
       /   \
      H     H
    ```

2. CS$_2$

    ```
    ..        ..
    :S = C = S:
    ```

3. I$_2$

    ```
    ..    ..
    :I — I:
    ..    ..
    ```

4. CH$_3$Br

    ```
         H
         |
         C....H
       /   \
     :Br    H
    ```

5. BH$_3$

    ```
         H
         |
         B
       /   \
      H     H
    ```

6. HF   H—F:

Reporting the News

Kathleen Estep • High School Social Studies Teacher • Springfield, OH

Social Studies

Student Objectives

Students will be able to:
- identify and analyze current events at the national, state, and local levels.
- practice decision-making skills.
- develop group-process skills.
- develop higher-level thinking skills.

Materials Needed

Teacher:
- several newspapers, one for each student group

NOTE: If possible, supply all the groups with the same day's newspaper. However, different newspapers for different groups also will work for this activity.

Students:
- "Reporting the News" worksheet
- a newspaper
- paper
- pencil or pen

118

Lesson Activity Process

Clock 45–60 minutes.

The teacher will:

1. Divide the class into groups of five or six, and give each group a copy of the "Reporting the News" worksheet, along with a newspaper. Have students read through the job descriptions on the worksheet. Then lead a discussion in which students talk about which job seems most important, most appealing, and most glamorous.

2. Now tell the groups that, for the next 20 minutes, they are to assume one of the television news team's roles and simulate a meeting to prepare for the "News at 11," using stories covered in the papers.

3. Have the groups peruse the newspapers, choosing 12 stories they feel are newsworthy and prioritizing the stories according to importance. (Remind them that the News Director has the final word regarding story selection and order.) In addition, groups must decide how many stories should be about national news, about state and local news, and about sports.

4. When the groups have finished their assignment, have them share their story decisions with the class. A volunteer from each group can list the story ideas in order on the chalkboard, using one or two keywords for each story.

5. If all the groups have used newspapers from the same day, have students compare the lists and defend each group's choices and order. If the newspapers are from consecutive days, ask students to determine whether the same story appears in more than one list and whether that story's importance diminished from day to day.

Modifications for Students with Special Needs

- Have students read the news articles aloud.
- Ask others to summarize the newspaper's articles.
- Perform this lesson as a whole-class activity, rather than in groups.

Evaluation

Evaluate each group by its attention to task, successful group process, speed of decision making, and the listing/defense of its articles.

Tips for Success

- This activity can be used with any size class. In small classes, students can play more than one role; in large classes, groups can be used and roles shared.
- You can divide groups either by having students count off by fives or group by proximity.
- You may wish to discuss with students what place there is in broadcast news for human interest stories.

Additional Related Activities

1. If your assignment is longer than one day, tell students to watch a television news broadcast the night before this lesson begins. Ask students to keep a list of the stories covered during the show. Lead a discussion in which students talk about whether the stories were, in their opinion, newsworthy.

2. If your substitute assignment will last a week, you may want to consider having students assume the roles identified on the handout. Then students actually could write their news stories, rehearse, and perform a newscast for the class. If the school has video equipment available, you could videotape the newscasts for playback and criticisms later. Remind students that, to simulate a real television newscast, the video camera will not stop once it starts.

3. Lead a discussion comparing your town's local newscasters. Whom do the students like? Dislike? Whom do students trust? Why?

Notes for Next Time

Reporting the News

Name _____ Date _____ Class _____

Members of the Television News Team

News Director(s)
Organizes the program. Meets with Anchors and Reporters to decide what stories will be covered and in what order. Responsible for editing the stories and making decisions about commercials, music, and background art.

Anchor(s)
Acts as the host of the news program. Introduces reporters and reads part of the news on camera.

Reporter(s)
Selects stories with merit for presentation at news meeting. Makes suggestions, but the News Director will make the final decision as to what stories will be covered. Summarizes the stories, answering these questions: Who? What? When? Where? Why? How? Prepares for field reports and interviews.

Cameraperson
Sets up the camera and makes sure everything is ready to tape. Follows the directions of the News Director but is free to make suggestions. Does the actual taping.

Sports Reporter
Selects, writes, and reads sports stories.

Weather Specialist
Gives the weather report, including some national and some local weather.

Media Specialist
Thinks of ways to illustrate and enhance stories. Ideas must be approved by the News Director.

120

Practicing the Language

Mary L. Harthun • Staff Development Specialist • Phoenix, AZ

Student Objectives

Students will be able to:

- use the target language orally.
- practice question formation in the target language.
- present an oral description of a famous person.
- interact in pairs.

Materials Needed

Students:

- paper
- pen or pencil
- language dictionary or textbook

Lesson Activity Process

Clock 45 minutes.

The teacher will:

1. Ask students to think of a famous person, and write that person's name on a scrap of paper. Tell students that it is important to keep the name a secret.
2. Divide the class into pairs. Explain that one student in each pair will try to guess the identity of the other student's famous person by asking questions in the target language, such as, "¿Es americano?" (Spanish) or "Est-il américain?" (French) (Is this person an American?)
3. Explain that students must only ask "yes or no" questions. Answers also should be given in the target language. In addition, students are limited to 20 questions, before the partner reveals the name of the famous person he or she chose.
4. Now give students five minutes in which to compose some questions privately.
5. Have pairs begin. After one member of the pair has made 20 guesses or correctly guessed the name, students should switch roles and repeat steps 3 and 4.
6. After this oral exercise, ask each student to write a paragraph in the target language, explaining why the person chosen is famous.
7. Have students share what they have written.

Modifications for Students with Special Needs

- Conduct as a whole-class activity, rather than in pairs.

- Allow student to use a typewriter, computer, or a dictaphone to record questions.
- Pair each student with a peer helper.

Evaluation

Students' written descriptions can serve for evaluation purposes. You may also decide to collect students' lists of questions to use as part of the evaluation.

Tips for Success

- Play the game once with the entire class, using, for example, Queen Elizabeth II as the famous person. Students might ask, "Are you living?" "Male?" "In politics?" "American?" and so on.
- Write 30 names of famous people on 3x5 cards for the students to select rather than thinking of them on their own. These cards could be used from class to class and carried in your survival kit.
- If the class has an odd number of students, create a group of three. In this case, two students will ask their questions of the third, then a different pair will ask its questions of a third, and so on.
- As students formulate their questions, walk around the room offering suggestions and helping students use language dictionaries and textbooks.

Additional Related Activities

1. Have students list, in the target language, five adjectives that describe their famous person.
2. Play 20 questions again, but this time limit students' famous person choices to people whose native language is (or was) the target language.
3. If you will be substituting for several days, have each student research and write, in the target language, a report on the life of his or her famous person. Have students share what they have learned with the class.

Notes for Next Time

121

Improving Fitness with Ultimate Frisbee

M. Linda Nickson • High School Physical Education Teacher • Stow, OH

Physical Education

Student Objectives

Students will be able to:

- develop accurate passing (throwing) and catching (receiving) skills.
- discover strategies to create and use open space (getting away from the defender).
- demonstrate the tactic of maintaining possession of the Frisbee.
- work together, call plays, and take responsibility for fair play.

Materials Needed

Teacher:

- stopwatch
- cones to mark the goal area
- jerseys or Pinnees for half the class
- Frisbee for each student pair

NOTE: This activity will need to take place on an outdoor playing field or in the gymnasium.

Students:

- a copy of "Improving Fitness with Ultimate Frisbee" worksheet

Lesson Activity Process

Clock 45–60 minutes.

The teacher will:

1. Distribute copies of the "Improving Fitness with Ultimate Frisbee" worksheet.
2. Explain that students will exercise in 30-second intervals, with 5 seconds of rest in between. During the first 30-second interval, students will perform one exercise of their choice from the worksheet's Cardiovascular Activities list. During the 5-second rest interval, students should choose their next activity from the Muscular Strength and Endurance Activities list.
3. Tell students to alternate from cardiovascular exercises to muscular strength and endurance exercises for 16 intervals.
4. Have a student volunteer time the intervals on the stopwatch. At the end of each 30-second activity or 5-second rest period, have the student call out, "Time." The volunteer should repeat this cycle 16 times.
5. When warm-ups are finished, ask volunteers to demonstrate throwing a Frisbee. Point out these throwing techniques:
   - shoulder to target.
   - step to target.
   - snap wrist on release.
6. Now direct the class to watch a volunteer catch the Frisbee. Point out these catching techniques:
   - thumb up if Frisbee is below chest.
   - thumb down if Frisbee is above chest.
   - watch Frisbee into hands.
   - relax fingers and hands.
   - pull Frisbee to body.
7. Divide the class into pairs and have one member of the pairs get a Frisbee, then find some playing space. Direct one student in each pair to sit, while the other stands 10 feet away.
8. Have the students in each pair pass the Frisbee back and forth, working for control and accuracy. Ask students to count the number of successful and consecutive passes they complete in a five-minute play period.
9. Now combine each pair with another, for a two versus two situation. Have each group of four students use cones to mark out a playing field that measures approximately 20' x 20'. The object is for one team to complete five consecutive passes to each other without losing possession to the other team. Each team will receive two points for every five completed passes.
10. Bring two four-member groups together, for a four versus four situation. Distribute jerseys to one team. Explain to all the students that Ultimate Frisbee combines tactics of football, basketball, and soccer. Ask volunteers to use cones to set end zones. Then ask students to read the objectives and rules of the game from the worksheet. Review any questions they may have.
11. Allow students to play out the game.

122

Modifications for Students with Special Needs

- Use a flippy flyer rather than a Frisbee.
- Ask the student to be responsible for timing the warm-up and rest periods.
- Ask the student to judge or referee.
- Have everyone play Frisbee using his or her nondominant hand.

Evaluation

Base your evaluation on observation of play and on student responses to these questions when play is over:
1. What must you do in this game to be successful? (keep possession)
2. How can players without the Frisbee help the player who has it? (be in a position to receive a pass)
3. Where should players go to get open? (away from the defense)
4. What do players need to do to advance the Frisbee? (pass quickly, set up, and pass between the defenders)

Tips for Success

- Circulate among the students as they warm up and then begin their Frisbee play to encourage and reinforce students' appropriate activities.
- Prepare a music cassette, with 30 seconds of music followed by a 5-second silent rest interval, repeated for a total of 16 music/rest intervals. This cassette would replace the stopwatch for warm-up exercises.
- Remind students that this is a time to learn, not a time to criticize.
- Reinforce examples of proper (or fair) game play.
- Play the game as eight versus eight or half the class versus half the class. Or you can change the number of players per team to adjust to skill level, or change the playing area, making it either smaller or larger. In addition, groups of three can be used if the class has an odd number of students.

Additional Related Activities

1. Ultimate Frisbee can be played with a football, foam disc, or other type of ball.
2. Have students attempt each of the warm-up activities on the handout. Then ask them to choose their favorite and use it to exercise for two minutes.

123

Notes for Next Time

Improving Fitness with Ultimate Frisbee

Name _____   Date _____ Class _____

Warm-Up Exercises

Cardiovascular Activities
Power Walk
Jog
Jog and Clap
Skip
Gallop
Hop
Bench Step
Line Jumping

Muscular Strength and Endurance Activities
Sit-Ups, Crunches, Obliques, Curls, Reverse Curls
Floor Push-ups
Wall Push-ups
Crab Walk
Power 1/2 Jacks

124

Ultimate Frisbee Rules

The object of the game is to work the Frisbee down field and pass to a teammate who is in position in the opponent's end zone.

1. The disc may never be handed—it must always be thrown.
2. No player may move while in possession of the disc.
3. The disc may be thrown in any direction.
4. No more than one person may guard a thrower.
5. The defensive team gains possession of the disc whenever the offensive team's pass is incomplete, intercepted, knocked down, or goes out of bounds.
6. Out-of-bounds throws are taken over by the opposing team at the point where the disc goes out of bounds. If this is in the end zone area, the throws may be taken from either corner of the end zone.
7. One point is scored for each Frisbee caught within the opponent's end zone. Play will continue until one team reaches a score of 10.

Analyzing Rehearsals

Dan Bruce • Choral Director • Pullman, WA

Student Objectives

Students will be able to:

- develop enthusiasm for the idea of trying to impress the choir director with improvement made in the music while he or she was gone.
- develop critical listening and performance skills.
- apply previously learned choral improvement techniques to the current rehearsal.
- practice leadership and participation skills.
- interpret music creatively.

Materials Needed

Students:

- copies of the music they are presently practicing
- one copy of "Analyzing Rehearsals" worksheet for a student recorder
- pencil for the student recorder

Lesson Activity Process

Clock 45–50 minutes.
The teacher will:

1. Select a student recorder and give him or her the "Analyzing Rehearsals" worksheet to complete as the activity progresses. Explain that the worksheet will be a report to the regular teacher of the class's accomplishments.
2. Elect a student director. Point out that this person must take the job seriously, be respected by the group, and be one of the more knowledgeable students in music in the class. Rotate this position several times during the rehearsal.
3. The student director will select a piece of music on which to work and will direct students as they sing the song the way they were taught.
4. Now ask students to suggest ways in which they feel the performance of the music will be improved. List student suggestions on the chalkboard.
5. Have the student director lead the group in implementing each suggestion, one at a time and one line at a time. It may take several times through the phrase or piece to practice or implement the suggestion.
6. Lead the group in a brief discussion about the effectiveness of the new performance. Did the song sound better the new way? Did everyone effectively incorporate the suggested idea? Which suggestion most improved the music?
7. Go on to a new phrase, section, or piece and repeat the process above.

Modifications for Students with Special Needs

- Begin with simple suggestions, such as speed, loudness, and so on.
- Allow students to sing the selection several times, so the difference becomes more obvious.
- Allow the student to choose the music for the class.

Evaluation

Student participation in class is the primary criterion for evaluation.

Tips for Success

- If the rehearsal seems to be going slowly, the substitute teacher may try to stimulate thinking (and listening) by suggesting these areas for consideration. The substitute teacher need not know all of the terms listed below, but hopefully the students know them:
  1. Do we have all the right notes?
  2. What about dynamics? (louds and softs)
  3. Are we using effective vocal production techniques? (posture, breath support, dropped jaw, etc.)
  4. How is our pronunciation? (open vowels, crisp consonants, clear word endings)
  5. Can the substitute teacher understand our words?
  6. Are we breathing in good places? (not in the middle of words or breaking up phrases, etc.)
  7. Are we in tune? If not, how can we improve the intonation?
     - Make sure the choir works on only one suggestion at time.
     - If no one volunteers any suggestions, ask a specific student for his or her input. Try to keep the rehearsal moving and the students involved.

125

Additional Related Activities

1. Ask the group to perform its practiced pieces for you. Because most audiences are made up of nonmusic people, a nonmusic substitute will be perfect for coming up with suggestions for improvement that can be representative of an audience and thereby improve the performance.

2. Lead a discussion in which students talk about which song in their repertoire creates the greatest emotion as they sing.

3. Have the choir sing a phrase, then try to repeat the words back to the group accurately. This is not only a fun activity but also points out poor enunciation in the group.

Notes for Next Time

Analyzing Rehearsals

Name _____ **Date** _____ **Class** _____

Name of piece

Measure numbers / rehearsal letter / section being worked on

Suggestion (Student)

Did the suggestion improve the music?

Explain.

Name of piece

Measure numbers / rehearsal letter / section being worked on

Suggestion (Student)

Did the suggestion improve the music?

Explain.

Name of piece

Measure numbers / rehearsal letter / section being worked on

Suggestion (Student)

Did the suggestion improve the music?

Explain.

Name of piece

Measure numbers / rehearsal letter / section being worked on

Suggestion (Student)

Did the suggestion improve the music?

Explain.

Constructing a House

Betsey Moore • Performance Consultant • Mount Holly, NJ

Industrial Technology

Student Objectives

Students will be able to:

- design a "theme" birdhouse.
- compile a list of construction materials.
- write a how-to instruction sheet.
- critique a partner's instructions.

Materials Needed

Students:

- unlined and lined paper
- measuring tools (ruler, compass)
- pencil

Lesson Activity Process

Clock 45–50 minutes.

The teacher will:

1. Introduce the concept of a "theme" birdhouse, which is being used now as a major fundraising technique for charity auctions. Architects, celebrities, and sports heroes are asked to construct birdhouses that are then auctioned off.

2. Tell students they are to think of a "theme" birdhouse design—perhaps based on a movie, video, book, or historic building or event. Each student is to think of his or her own "theme." The assignment is to draw the design, compile a list of required building materials, and write an instruction sheet on how to build the birdhouse.

3. Allow 10 minutes at the end of the class for students to share their designs with a partner who is responsible for a critique—not of the design but of the materials list and the construction directions.

Modifications for Students with Special Needs

- Have students work in teams to create their theme birdhouses.
- Create the birdhouse plans as a class.
- Provide a visual model for students to use as reference.

Evaluation

Each student will hand in the design, the materials list, and the construction instructions, which are evaluated based on thoroughness, clarity, and appropriateness.

Tips for Success

- Do not take in pictures of birdhouses—they might bias students' design decisions.
- Tell students they have 30 minutes in which to complete their assignments. Then give them time checks every 5–10 minutes, so that they will be better time managers.
- *World Book Encyclopedia,* Volume B, "Bird," has a section on building a birdhouse, if you wish to use the measurements recommended there as a reference. In addition, the school library might have a book with birdhouse-building instructions.

Additional Related Activities

1. If you will be substituting in this position for several days, supply students with the materials their plans require, and allow them to build their birdhouses. If this is the case, you may want them to create more formal plans on graph paper before beginning their building projects.

2. Ask students for theme ideas for birdhouses. List suggestions on the chalkboard. Then have students vote for their favorite theme. Have all the students draw just the front of a birdhouse illustrating the chosen theme. Ask them to share their finished drawings with the class.

Notes for Next Time

128

Mapping Concepts

Jan Fall • K–12 Gifted and Talented Coordinator • Rochester, MN
Jan Smith • High School English and Reading Teacher • Rochester, MN

Critical Thinking

Student Objectives

Students will be able to:

- use a graphic organizer to activate prior knowledge and/or learning.
- synthesize concepts into a holistic picture.
- develop thinking skills.
- provide a structure for organization of data.
- identify common themes and concepts and differentiate main ideas and supporting details.

Materials Needed

Students:

- pen or pencil
- a copy of the "Mapping Concepts" worksheet

Lesson Activity Process

Clock 45–50 minutes.

The teacher will:

1. Explain that the students will use a strategy that will help them review prior knowledge by organizing information.
2. Distribute the "Mapping Concepts" worksheets. Draw a copy of the concept map on the worksheet on the chalkboard and explain the structure of the map. The main topic, concept, or theme should be placed in the center of the map. The spokes, or "legs," will identify main ideas that further describe the topic or theme. Finally, accompanying details will be placed adjacent to each main idea "leg."
3. In the center of the map, put the words, "Downhill Skiing." Now ask the students to help you complete the map. The finished map might look something like this:

4. After completing the sample concept map, check for questions or comments.
5. Explain that the blank map given in the handout should not restrict students to a certain number of "legs" and/or details. Instead, it should be seen as a conceptual framework from which to develop a map of connecting ideas.
6. When it is clear that the students understand the mapping process, ask them to list 5–10 topics, concepts, and/or themes that they may have studied in class—e. g., a novel, a period of history, etc.
7. Each student or group of students will select a topic from the list on the board. On the worksheet, students will create their own map using the topics they have selected.

Modifications for Students with Special Needs

- Choose one topic from those listed on the chalkboard and complete it together as a class.
- Pair the student with a peer helper to complete the worksheet.

Evaluation

Evaluate the worksheets for content and understanding.

Answers to Student Handout

Answers will vary according to the topics chosen.

Tips for Success

- The mapping process can work for any content area. It allows the students to develop thinking skills within the context of a particular content area. If this lesson is used at the beginning of a school year, have students recall concepts from the previous year. At the end of a unit of study, it provides an excellent review.
- Many students at the secondary level have had exposure to graphic organizers and may be able to add more insight to the process. They should be encouraged to try new organizers. Knowing about many different types will allow them to select more appropriate ways to conceptualize data.
- Students may work individually or in groups, whichever is more comfortable. If students are

129

mapping individually, encourage them to select a topic with which they may have had difficulty.

- It may be difficult for a substitute who is unfamiliar with content to give guidance on fine-tuning a concept map. Therefore, it is a good idea to leave some time at the end of class for students to share the maps they have created. This also serves as a review for all the class members, and concepts may be challenged or enhanced by other students.
- Encourage students to add to their map designs and/ or illustrations that could serve as mnemonic devices.

Additional Related Activities

1. When a new topic is going to be introduced, a concept map is a good way to assess students' prior knowledge.

2. Have students use their finished map to complete a writing assignment, using the map's theme as the composition's theme. Tell students to use the points they made to complete their concept maps as points in their writing. The organization of the map allows a natural flow of ideas into paragraphs and sequences.

3. Character maps can be developed in the same manner as a concept map to describe characters read about or characters that are being created by the students.

4. Have students do a concept map of themselves. Direct them to include things that are important in their lives—i.e., school, friends, family, extra-curricular activities, the future, etc.

5. Concept maps can be used as an evaluation tool. Given a list of related ideas, students would create a map indicating their level of understanding of the topic.

Notes for Next Time

Critical Thinking Student Page

Mapping Concepts

Name _____ Date _____ Class _____

Follow the teacher's instructions to complete your concept map below.

Concept Map

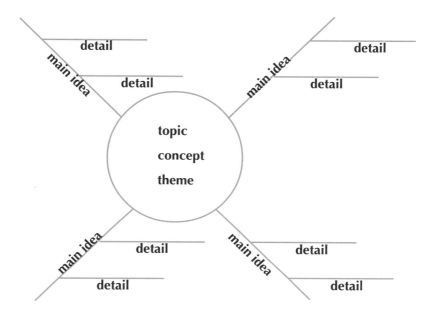

Concept Map

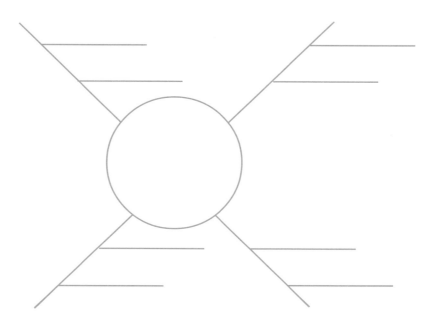

Chapter 8

Ensuring Success

Your success at being a substitute teacher, while dependent on many factors, is within your control. In addition to your effectiveness with students in the classroom, your success is linked to your professionalism, evaluations of your performance, and following school board policies and federal and state laws concerning educational settings.

When you are in the classroom as a substitute teacher, you represent the school and the district to students, their parents, and, thus, the general public. Your behavior as a substitute teacher must reflect the professionalism characteristic of a teacher on staff. How you handle confidential information about district students and teachers and how you communicate with parents and the community, for example, demonstrate your personal and professional ethics. As a professional, it is imperative that you know the responsibilities inherent in having access to such confidential information. Therefore, you must consider up front—before accepting this responsibility—where your loyalty lies: to the children you teach and the educators with whom you work or to your friends, acquaintances, and neighbors.

Another way that you guarantee success as a substitute teacher is to work tenaciously at evaluating your performance, seeking the evaluation of others, and taking action to improve your skills. When you can objectively critique your own actions, accept the criticism of professionals you may not know very well, determine what changes must be made, and then begin to make them, your skills have the potential to reach mature levels. School administrators notice this type of improvement, and you will become a viable asset to the district.

Success also hinges on whether you understand the very basic structure of educational systems in the United States and the laws that govern them. Basic legal guidelines in educational settings, including those concerning teacher and student rights, center around areas such as discrimination, speech and free expression, corporal punishment, suspension and expulsion, religion, child abuse, and sexual harassment. It is important that you understand your protected rights as a teacher and how to take preventive measures in avoiding liability.

Professionalism

To be successful, you must be committed to your role as a substitute teacher, which is challenging because more is required of a substitute than most people realize. How easy it would be just to go in, tell the students what to do, then sit and watch them do it, maintaining order if you have to! Reality shows that you will be confronted with many tasks that never allow you to sit and do personal projects while on duty.

Substitutes are professionals who step into the regular teacher's classroom, assuming his or her responsibilities and demands in carrying out programs outlined by district curriculum and faculty. They may step into any classroom situation: kindergarten through 12th grade; self-contained class, departmentalized and individualized class, or one with cooperative teams; gifted and talented class or a special needs resource room; or "special" classes such as physical education, industrial technology, art, vocational agriculture, or computer science. Substitutes must also accept extra duties that staff teachers perform such as lunchroom or bus duty or playground supervision. Commitment and professionalism are obviously essential.

The primary objective of the school district is to provide the best educational program possible. It is important for you to be committed to this objective. The community and the school administration expect all school personnel to follow appropriate patterns of behavior based on professional and ethical codes that reflect commonly accepted community standards.

Substitutes must establish an ethical and professional relationship with faculty, staff, and students. For

example, you should be friendly in the staff lounge and lunchroom but not pushy or gossipy. Maintaining a positive attitude toward all teaching assignments is another key to successful substituting. Staff and students alike are more likely to accept a substitute teacher with a friendly and cooperative attitude.

Public Relations

Every educational system works hard to maintain a positive image in the community for both the system as a whole and individual schools. You can be an important player in establishing good or poor impressions in the community. As a member of the community who knows the schools well, you can serve as a good public relations ambassador by sharing what the schools need without divulging private confidences. After all, when you are shopping in the local grocery store, you never know who you will see—students, parents, teachers, or influential community leaders such as school board members. As a substitute, you have become a part of the district's educational community and must respect and be loyal to your employer.

Professional Courtesy

133

Your general attitude and behavior should exhibit professional courtesy to the teacher whose duties you are completing as well as to other staff members. Though the substitute is not hired as a custodian, remember that you are a guest in that classroom and must, therefore, leave it at least in the same condition as it was when you entered. If you find the desks in groups of four and you prefer rows, be sure to return them to groups of four at the end of your stay. In addition to being good protocol, it is just considerate to leave the classroom in better condition than it was when you arrived—paper picked up, desks straight, chalkboards clean, and student work neatly organized for the teacher's return.

In some schools, staff members are paired in teaching teams who collaborate on schedules and share responsibility for the same group(s) of students during a particular time block. If such is the case with your day's assignment, you may wish to ask the other team members about the general courtesies that members follow in their team. Respecting existing relationships and accommodating specifics will also add to your success as a substitute.

Professional Attire

Though attire varies from district to district, community to community, or even from one part of the country to another, your school assignment dictates what you wear any given day. Even though schools may belong to the same district, each school has its own character and often has its own written or unwritten dress code for students and teachers. Your observations of what the dress code might be are certainly important, but still ask someone on the campus what is appropriate. Common sense is the best rule, but keep in mind that some classes require special types of clothes—slacks for kindergarten classes where sitting on the floor is part of the routine, lab coats for science class, shorts for physical education, work clothes for an industrial technology class, etc.

If you are not familiar with the school and are unable to check with the school secretary or principal ahead of time, remember that first appearances are important, so dress conservatively. For women, professional attire is a stylish blouse and dress slacks, a tailored dress, or a suit; for men, slacks and a dress shirt with a tie are appropriate. After that first school visit, you can then modify your attire to fit the campus norm.

Because teachers are on their feet most of the day, remember substitutes should wear shoes suitable for hard, slippery floors or carpeted areas. Because schools are not always carpeted, a non-slip sole is a wise choice. Unless gym shoes are required, dress shoes with low heels are most appropriate.

Evaluating Your Performance

Excellent teachers seek ways to improve their lessons, finding new ways to perfect their craft so students can grow and learn more productively. In Chapter 3, you learned about providing feedback to the regular teacher about how the school day went—lessons accomplished, student performance and discipline issues, and homework assigned. However, it is just as important for you to evaluate your own performance as well as receive feedback from those with whom you work—students, the regular teacher, and school administrators.

Self-Evaluation

An experienced teacher knows when he or she has done an adequate job or a superb job, but it helps to have some kind of yardstick by which to measure. The school district may complete some kind of evaluation, but it is always best to critique your own performance at the end of the day or within 24 hours of the assignment. It is important for you to reflect on what went well and what you would like to do differently the next time you have a similar teaching assignment.

Some schools have a form for the regular classroom teacher to fill out to evaluate substitutes' performance. If so, request a copy each time you accept an assignment and complete it as a self-evaluation after you have concluded the assignment. When you receive the teacher's form, you can compare how you thought you did against how well you fulfilled the regular teacher's expectations.

The Self-Evaluation Form on page 135 might prove helpful for a quick assessment. Its checklist includes items such as arriving on time, maintaining normal classroom discipline, leaving the classroom in good order, and maximizing student learning. The form might end with unfinished sentences to be completed about areas that you will want to remember the next time you go to the same school or classroom.

A more abbreviated form is the Substitute Assignment Log on page 14, which records important data about your assignments: date, school, contact person, teacher, and grade or courses. It has limited space for notes to help you remember the experience, so if the log is too brief, you might create a binder that opens with the log. After the log use filler paper to write a narrative about each assignment's activities, possible suggestions for improvement, or ideas obtained from other teachers. Dividers can be used to set off the categorized information for easier use as you refer to it later or gather new information to add to your notebook.

Professional and Student Evaluation

Sometimes the district or school administration has

Self-Evaluation Form

Yes	No	
❏	❏	I arrived on time.
❏	❏	I was able to organize my day before having to begin my duties.
❏	❏	I was able to familiarize myself with the lesson(s).
❏	❏	I was friendly and professional throughout the day.
❏	❏	I was able to contact the regular teacher(s).
❏	❏	I carried out the regular teacher's plan so student learning was maximized.
❏	❏	I left the classroom in a neat and orderly condition.
❏	❏	I left follow-up feedback for the regular teacher(s).
❏	❏	I would like to return to this school.

I can improve my substitute experience by:

The most interesting event of the day was:

135

What I enjoyed most about today was:

Today's Date: **School:**   **Grade(s) Taught:**

Subject(s)   **# of Classes:**   **Expected Pay:**

Other Duties Performed:

Additional Comments:

Administrator's and Teacher's Evaluation of the Substitute

Date:

Substitute's Name_____ for _____(Teacher's Name)

The principal should make at least one classroom visit per day. After the principal has written comments, this form should be placed in the mailbox of the classroom teacher to be completed and returned to the office. When a substitute is used regularly in a building, the principal need not fill out an evaluation form each time the substitute is employed.

A. Principal's Comments:

1. The substitute interacted with the students in a professional manner.

2   The substitute maintained a positive, orderly classroom climate.

3. The substitute carried out the regular teacher's lesson plans to maximize student learning.

4. Other.

136

B. Regular Teacher's Comments:

1. The substitute followed the lesson plans that were available.

2. The substitute indicated in some way which plans were carried out and which were left to be completed.

3. The substitute maintained the classroom.

4. The substitute left a fairly detailed and explicit account of significant things that happened during the day— parent visitation, child injury, etc.

5. The substitute corrected appropriate assignments.

6. The substitute is recommended for continued reemployment.

designated a particular person to conduct teacher evaluation, and this person may also be responsible for evaluating substitute teachers. It could be the principal, assistant principal, level or department chair, or a staff development specialist. Administrative personnel might provide feedback to the substitute in one of several ways. The assistant principal might just drop into the classroom to see how things are going, schedule a conference with you at the end of the school day, or complete a school or district feedback form similar to the Principal and Teacher Substitute Evaluation Form on page 136. A copy of the completed report is usually kept in the school principal's records and possibly the district personnel files. It is common practice for the district's or school's secretary to make a copy of the evaluation report and send it to the substitute teacher.

When you receive a written or oral evaluation from a school staff member, remember that he or she gives you this information to help you become a stronger teacher for the school's students and an asset to the district, one it will call upon frequently. If the evaluation has major negative concerns, it could result in your being assigned only to other campuses within the same district or not being called anymore. Upon receipt of the evaluation report, if you wish to discuss the report in person, contact the school principal. You are also generally permitted to submit to the district or principal's office in writing any comments pertinent to the evaluation for inclusion in your personnel file. Administrators who need permanent teachers often start by reviewing the district's files of exemplary substitute teachers.

If a standard evaluation form or process is not used in the school where you are assigned, develop your own form or duplicate the Substitute Evaluation Form provided on page 138, leaving it and a stamped, self-addressed envelope with the school secretary, asking the regular teacher and/or principal to evaluate your work and send you the requested feedback. Knowing what impact you had on the students during your stay can also add to your success as a substitute. Providing students an evaluation form is an easy matter. It must not be long, and the activity should consume 10 minutes or less, or it could preempt the real purpose of the day—to learn. The Student Substitute Evaluation on page 140 provides a model for gaining student feedback, or you can create your own.

Legal Guidelines

In the last 20 years, legal issues have played an important part in the lives of students and teachers. New laws and landmark cases have added to the legal responsibilities of teachers. A substitute teacher is as legally responsible for students, equipment, and materials assigned to his or her supervision as is the regular teacher who is replaced. Each school district has board of education policies, regulations, and procedures that are unique to the school district. In addition, state statutes, federal mandates, and court decisions guide decisions teachers make every day in the classroom. As a substitute teacher, you are legally responsible under these same laws. Many laws relate specifically to education, and a far greater number apply to the public generally but indirectly affect schools because students and teachers are part of the public.

Laws affecting education come from federal and state governments. The Tenth Amendment to the U.S. Constitution makes education a state function, while the First Amendment ensures basic personal freedom and civil rights. In addition, the Fourteenth Amendment defines citizenship and specifies that "due process" should be followed in guaranteeing the rights of citizenship. Fourteenth Amendment cases have involved saluting the U.S. flag, rights of parents, racial segregation, teacher dismissal, and student discipline.

Some recent Supreme Court decisions have upheld random drug testing of school athletes, the disciplining of students for "vulgar and offensive" speech, and administrator authority to censure student-authored articles in school newspapers. The Supreme Court has not supported, through its recent decisions, clergy-led prayer at high school graduation or convocations when invited by the school administration and denial of access to student-sponsored religious groups if access is provided to other student groups not directly related to the school's curriculum.

137

Substitute Evaluation

Date of Evaluation _____   **Campus**

Substitute's Name _____ **for** _____ **(Teacher's Name)**

Personal Characteristics	Outstanding	Good	Average	Unsatisfactory	Not Observed
Attitude					
Interactions with Students					
Interactions with Staff					
Punctuality					
Reliability					
Teaching Characteristics					
Knowledge of Field					
Instructional Delivery					
Ability to Follow Teacher's Plan					
Handling of Materials and Equipment					
Classroom Management Skills					

138

Handling of Records

Yes   **No**

❏   ❏   1. The substitute left a fairly detailed and explicit account of significant things that happened during the day—parent contact, student injury, etc.

❏   ❏   2. The "Feedback to Regular Teacher" form was completed and left for the regular teacher.

❏   ❏   3. The substitute is recommended for continued reemployment at this campus.

4. Additional Comments:

Signature of Evaluator _____ Position _____

This form is to be completed by any of the following: Principal, Assistant Principal, Department Chair, Staff Development Specialist

State legislatures have enacted the most laws affecting public schools. In most cases, states have placed the authority to adopt and enforce reasonable rules and regulations for the operation and management of the public school system in the hands of local boards of education, school administrators, and classroom teachers.

Given today's emphasis on student and educator rights and varied responsibilities and legal solutions for the conflicts among students, teachers, and administrators, examining more closely the legal issues you may confront as a substitute would be a wise investment of your time. Taking a university course on school law, searching the *Education Index* or the ERIC database at the library for professional journal articles that summarize in lay terminology the important points of such legislation and important cases, contacting a school-board attorney, or reading any number of books available on the subject (see the bibliography on pages 149–50) are possible options. Student and teacher rights and preventing tort liability are important areas in which teachers should develop an awareness of current law and district procedures.

Teacher Rights

The legal relationship between the teacher and the school district depends on various sources of law, including the constitutional rights and freedoms of the teacher as a citizen, state statutes governing public schools, and contract provisions between the governing board and the educator. In many states, courts have held that school board policy and personnel manuals are incorporated into the employment contract. In addition, specific statutes in your state or local board of education policies or regulations may govern the employment and conduct of substitute teachers. Legal information pertaining specifically to substitute teachers can be obtained by reviewing the state school code at the local library or by requesting information from the state department of education and the department of teacher certification. Some of the legal issues affecting teachers' rights include speech and expression, personal appearance and dress codes, union activities, academic freedom in the classroom, personal freedoms and privacy, and due process related to

teacher employment and dismissal.

Speech and Expression. Courts have held that a teacher may not be disciplined for speaking as a citizen upon matters of public concern unless the teacher's interest in such speech is outweighed by a reasonable belief on the part of the school district that the speech would disrupt the school environment, undermine the authority of the administrator to supervise, or destroy close working relationships. The form, content, and context of any given statement are considered to determine whether a teacher's speech addressed a matter of public concern. The U.S. Supreme Court in *Pickering v. Board of Education*, 1968, held that, "absent proof of false statement knowingly or recklessly made by him, a teacher's exercise of his right to speak on issues of public importance may not furnish the basis for his dismissal from public employment." Constitutionally protected speech does not entitle a teacher to be excessively critical and derisive of duly constituted school authority and to denounce and abuse other teachers personally, as detailed in a Kentucky court case, *Amburgey v. Cassady*, 1974. In another court case, an Ohio teacher was terminated by the school board for calling a radio station and criticizing a memorandum to teachers relating to teacher dress and appearance and public support for bond issues. In this case—*Mt. Healthy City District Board of Education v. Doyle*, 1977—the U.S. Supreme Court held that the communication by the teacher was protected by the First and Fourteenth Amendments of the U.S. Constitution. The teacher was dismissed on other grounds, including arguments with other school employees, obscene gestures to two students, and other incidents of employment not related to protected speech.

Personal Appearance and Dress Codes. Generally, school dress codes and personal grooming requirements have been upheld by the courts as long as they are reasonable and do not infringe on the free speech rights of teachers. Most courts will not overturn school policy related to dress codes for teachers nor substitute its judgment for that of the board unless the board's actions are clearly unreasonable and arbitrary. If the board's rules are to enhance the professional image of its teachers in the view of students and parents, the rules are likely to be upheld.

Student Substitute Evaluation

Directions: Briefly (25–50 words per question) answer the following questions regarding your substitute experience.

1. **How did the class period go?**

2. **In what way(s) did you contribute to making the classroom a positive experience?**

3. **What will you do differently next time?**

4. **How would you describe the behavior of your classmates?**

5. **If there were any mix-ups, what caused them?**

140

6. **What should the substitute have done differently?**

7. **Assuming that you are a substitute teacher, how will you "instruct" your students to maximize learning?**

8. **What can I do in the future to improve your substitute experience?**

9. **Additional comments:**

Union Activities. Teachers have a constitutional right to join a union. Whether they have a right to engage in collective bargaining, however, depends on state laws. The law in each state varies. Some state laws allow only for teachers' organizations to "meet and confer" with school boards, while other state laws may require the board of education to meet with representatives of the teachers' organization to negotiate specified benefits. A teacher cannot be terminated if the termination is based on participation in union activities.

Academic Freedom. Teachers often ask such questions as: "Can I talk about religion in the classroom? Can I choose supplemental materials and books or films to use in my classroom instruction? Do I have to inform the principal if I use a guest speaker?" Many of these issues involve academic freedom and, while these activities may be within the protection of the First Amendment, there have been limitations imposed by state statutes, school board policies, practices and procedures in the school district, and court decisions.

Academic freedom of teachers is balanced against the competing educational values of the school district and the community. Short-term substitutes generally do not face this problem, as they have one or two days' lesson plans left for them, or can use the ones in Chapters 5, 6, and 7. If you are a long-term substitute, review the district's approved list of textbooks, supplementary materials, software, and guest speakers.

Generally, if teaching materials are age appropriate, relevant to the subject in a board-approved curriculum, and do not materially and substantially interfere with school discipline, they may be used unless specifically prohibited by the school district's governing board. Courts have ruled that when classroom methods are "conducted within the ambit of professional standards" and teacher statements in class neither substantially interfere with student discipline nor subject students to unfair indoctrination, then a teacher may not be fired for discussing controversial issues, as in *Sterzing v. Ft. Bend Independent School District*, 1974. However, in *Birdwell v. Hazelwood School District*, 1974, a St. Louis teacher was dismissed because his statements to his math class were "completely irrelevant" and "diverted the time and attention of both students and

teacher from the prescribed curriculum." Teachers have been dismissed for using vulgar words "particularly when no academic or educational purpose can possibly be served"—as was the case in *Celestine v. Lafayette Parish School Board*, 1973—and for not obeying a directive from the school principal to stop discussing school politics, to teach economics, and to use more conventional teaching methods. In a recent case, in which two teachers resigned, junior high school students were allowed to bring personal videotapes for group viewing while the teachers prepared grade reports. One of the videotapes was rated "R" and was not appropriate for the age of the students. Even though the current trend of the courts is to be less intrusive in academic issues, it is advisable for the substitute to discuss use of any books, articles, computer software, films, or guest speakers with the principal and ask for an approved list of texts or supplemental materials if the substitute intends to continue substitute teaching in a particular school or district over an extended period of time.

Privacy outside the Classroom. Historically, teachers have been held to higher public standards of conduct and fewer personal freedoms than citizens in nonteaching professions. Recently, however, state tenure laws, federal laws related to discrimination in the workplace, and significant court decisions supporting teachers who were challenging unreasonable dismissal actions have allowed teachers increased freedom to exercise their personal rights.

Generally, the personal beliefs, social or political philosophies, or associations of a teacher may not be restricted by statute or education board policy unless the private conduct of the teacher is criminal or disrupts the educational process or the teacher's effectiveness in the classroom. Teachers may exercise their personal and individual constitutional freedoms as any other citizen.

Due Process. General contract law applies to teachers' contracts with school districts. Teaching contracts may be entered into by mutual agreement of the teacher and the education board and must feature specific terms of employment, including the length of employment. If a substitute is terminated for cause by a public employer,

141

or prior to the expiration of the employment contract, he or she may be entitled to a due process hearing under the Fourteenth Amendment to the U.S. Constitution or the state constitution where the teacher resides. Most states have laws defining the due process rights of teachers and other school employees in addition to grievance procedures and due process rights conferred by education board policies.

Unless a teacher has tenure, the school board has no obligation to renew probationary or substitute teaching contracts beyond the ending date specified in the contract. Contracts can also be terminated by mutual agreement. The U.S. Supreme Court in *Board of Regents v. Roth*, 1972, held that a liberty interest under the Fourteenth Amendment is not implicated by a contract nonrenewal if a person's good name, reputation, honor, or integrity is not at stake, as there is no stigma that would foreclose future employment opportunities. Therefore, probationary, nontenured, and substi-

Supreme Court Decisions Affecting Teacher Employment

1967 Keyishian v. Board of Regents
Loyalty oaths that make mere membership in a subversive organization grounds for dismissal are unconstitutionally broad.

1968 Pickering v. Board of Education
Absent proof of false statements knowingly or recklessly made, teachers may not be dismissed for exercising the freedom to speak on matters of public concern.

1972 Board of Regents v. Roth **and** Perry v. Sindermann
These companion cases, decided at the same time by the Supreme Court, discuss the Court's view of what constitutes a property and liberty interest under the Fourteenth Amendment. A nontenured teacher does not have a property right to continued employment, and teachers may not be dismissed for public criticism of educational board policies or superiors if based on issues of public concern.

1976 Hortonville Joint School District No. 1 v. Hortonville Education Association
School board members may serve as impartial hearing officers in due process hearings unless clear bias can be substantiated.

1977 Mount Healthy City School District v. Doyle
When teachers are recommended for termination based on exercising First Amendment rights, they must show that the speech conduct was protected and was a substantial and motivating factor to dismiss for cause or not to renew the contract. The school district must prove that, absent the protected conduct, it would have reached the same decision.

1983 Connick v. Myers
Public employees do not have an unlimited guarantee of freedom of expression in public statements on matters of personal interest or specified employee-employer problems in the workplace.

1985 Cleveland Board of Education v. Louderville
Public employees who can be discharged only for cause must be afforded the pretermination opportunity to respond to oral or written notice of charges and a statement of the evidence against him or her, with provisions for a full-blown administrative hearing at a later date.

1986 Garland Independent School District v. Texas State Teachers Association
School mailboxes can be used by teachers to distribute union information and material.

1987 School Board of Nassau County v. Arline
Individuals having contagious diseases are considered handicapped and cannot be discriminated against in the workplace when the discriminatory acts are based solely on fear of contamination.

1991 Censonia Bd. of Educ. v. Philbrook
School boards are only bound to offer a fair and reasonable accommodation of teacher's religious needs.

tute teachers do not have a property or liberty interest claim to due process unless they are dismissed before the expiration of the teaching contract or unless the dismissal action impairs a fundamental constitutional right, creates a stigma, or damages the teacher's reputation to the extent that it forecloses other employment opportunities.

Some important Supreme Court cases affecting teachers' rights in matters of employment and in matters inside and outside the classroom are described in the chart on page 142.

Copyright. With increased use of technology in the schools, educators and school officials must have an awareness of copyright laws, rules, and rights of authors. Most school districts have guidelines for teachers related to copying materials for classroom use. For example, you may make a single copy of the following for use in preparation for teaching a class or your own research: a chapter from a book; an article from a periodical or newspaper; a short story, essay, or poem, whether or not from a collective work; charts, graphs, diagrams, cartoons, or pictures from a book, periodical, or newspaper.

You may make multiple copies for classroom use or discussion based upon "tests" of brevity, spontaneity, and cumulative effect. You may not photocopy workbooks, exercises, tests, and answer sheets to create consumable materials for a class, or copy materials as a substitute for the purchase of sheet music. If you plan to copy items for instructional use, you should ask the school principal for the school district's guidelines for copying materials for classroom use.

Adequate Supervision and Liability. Accidents involving students do happen at school and can occur in the classroom, hallway, playground, shop and physical education classes, on the school bus, and during field trips. Teachers often ask these questions: "Am I legally responsible if a student I'm supervising is injured? Am I liable if a student is injured when I leave the classroom?" Teacher liability is part of an area of law called torts. The theory of tort law involves the relationship between individuals and the right for an individual to be free from bodily injury, whether intentionally or carelessly caused by others.

In a school setting, teachers and other school employees may be held accountable under the law for negligence. Negligence is the type of tort most commonly filed against teachers, due to their direct contact with students on a daily basis and the teacher's duty to supervise. For a successful negligence action, certain prerequisites must be met:

1. The teacher must have a duty to the student.
2. The teacher must have failed to exercise a reasonable standard of care in his or her actions.
3. The teacher's actions must be the proximate (direct) cause of the injury to the student.
4. The student must prove that he or she suffered an actual injury.

Teachers have a contract or statutory duty to supervise students as an employee of the school district. If the teacher has acted as a "reasonable and prudent person" in the supervision of the student and the act causing the student injury was not foreseeable, the teacher will probably not be held liable for negligence. Educators have been held negligent in court cases involving failure to provide adequate supervision, permitting students to use unsafe equipment or play unsafe games, failure to give adequate warnings or safety instructions, taking unreasonable risks, or improperly supervised or organized field trips. Generally, districts and the public expect a greater standard of care for young children, disabled students, students in shop classes having potentially dangerous equipment, physical education classes (use of equipment and safety standards), science classes involving the use of chemicals, and off-campus school-sponsored activities. You should ask another teacher or school official the procedure to follow when you find it necessary to leave a classroom with students under your supervision and inquire as to the procedure for giving medication to students (even an aspirin). By being aware of potential safety hazards in classes, in the school, and on the playground, and anticipating problems that might arise on field trips, teachers may be able to prevent potential injuries to students and lessen tort liability claims against themselves as teachers.

143

Student Rights

Most of the important education-related litigation and political debate revolves around student rights, particularly related to discrimination, disciplinary actions, saluting the U.S. flag, student records, freedom of speech and religion, child abuse, and sexual harassment. Just as teachers must know and accommodate student rights, substitutes must also be aware of and protect the rights of students while at the same time protecting the best interests of the school district.

Discrimination and Equal Opportunity. A student may not be denied school admission based on race, gender, or handicap. The Civil Rights Act of 1964 and other laws on discrimination were designed to eliminate discrimination based on race, color, or national origin, while granting minority groups certain benefits or services. These benefits include: (1) providing services that are not available to majority groups; (2) grading the work of all students according to the same scale; and (3) following similar disciplinary practices as for majority students.

To prevent gender discrimination, the Civil Rights Act was amended in 1972 to require that no person be subjected to sex discrimination during any educational activity or program receiving federal funds. Title IX, as this amendment is called, requires that there be one set of rules for both genders on discipline, opportunities for activities, rules on appearance, and availability of counseling testing or guidance. In 1992, the U.S. Supreme Court in *Franklin v. Gwinnette Country Schools* ruled that public school students may sue, under Title IX, educational institutions for compensatory damages when teachers sexually harass students. Children with disabilities are protected within many laws. The Individuals with Disabilities Education Act of 1990 (IDEA), formerly known as Public Law 94–142 and the Education for All Handicapped Children Act, ensures a free and appropriate education in the least restrictive environment. Section 504 of the Rehabilitation Act of 1973 ensures that disabled persons are not subject to discrimination when enrolled in school districts receiving federal funds for programs. Some students with learning problems may require special assistance in the regular classroom to provide them with an equal opportunity to learn. Section 504 requires school districts to identify these students and provide such assistance as needed to ensure success in the regular classroom.

The Americans with Disabilities Act of 1990 became effective in 1992 and expands civil rights protection to individuals with disabilities to private sector employment, in addition to public services, public accommodations, transportation, and telecommunication. The law is applicable to all public entities, including school districts. This federal law is currently being used by parents and advocates of disabled students in the schools and has been viewed as an expansion of the Rehabilitation Act of 1973.

In 1974, Congress expanded coverage of the Bilingual Education Act of 1968 to address the needs of students with limited English proficiency from all income levels. The act also provides a more precise definition of the bilingual education program required in English and the child's native language to the extent needed for the child to make effective progress.

Speech and Expression. In *Tinker v. Des Moines Independent School District,* 1969, the Supreme Court ruled that schools could exercise authority over student disruption but must not restrict students' First Amendment speech rights, as long as they do not behave in a manner that disrupts the operation of the school or interferes with the rights of others. The case centered around wearing black armbands in protest against the Vietnam War.

The *Tinker* case contains one of the most important quotes by the U.S. Supreme Court in school law cases: "It can hardly be argued that either student or teachers shed their constitutional rights to freedom of speech or expression at the schoolhouse gate." In more recent years, however, the Supreme Court has given more support to school officials. In *Bethel School District v. Fraser,* 1986, the Court held that teachers and administrators can decide what type of speech in the classroom or in school assembly is appropriate and supported school officials suspending students for lewd or indecent speech. In a 1988 decision, the Supreme Court, in *Hazelwood School District v. Kuhlmeier,* determined that school officials can exercise "editorial control over the style and content of student speech in school-sponsored expressive activities so long as their actions are reasonably related to legitimate (educational) concerns."

Flag Salute and Pledge of Allegiance. The Supreme Court ruled in *West Virginia State Board of Education v. Barnette,* 1943, that the state cannot compel a student to salute the flag or participate in the Pledge of Allegiance if participation violates his or her values. Though students have the right to differ with others, they may not interfere with other students who do wish to participate.

Generally, the courts will not allow teachers to discipline students for not participating in the Pledge of Allegiance. In *Goetz v. Ansel,* 1973, the Second Circuit Court of Appeals decision struck down a regulation requiring a student who refused to salute the flag to either stand or leave his classroom. The student could not be compelled to participate in the pledge nor could he be punished for refusing to participate. The court pointed out that the conduct of the student caused no disruption of school activities, a situation which could have changed the decision. In a Massachusetts case, the state supreme court ruled that a statute requiring all teachers to lead the class in a group recitation of the pledge violated teachers' rights to free speech under the First Amendment to the U.S. Constitution.

Corporal Punishment. In *Ingraham v. Wright,* 1977, it was determined that administering discipline in the form of corporal punishment cannot be generalized into a policy but must be handled on an individual basis. Before corporal punishment is administered the following should be considered: the seriousness of the offense, the attitude and past behavior of the child, the nature and severity of the punishment, the age and strength of the child, and the availability of less severe but equally effective means of discipline.

Some states, however, specifically prohibit corporal punishment, and a few state legislatures leave the decision whether or not to use corporal punishment to each individual school district. The substitute must know the school district's policy on corporal punishment and determine if it is allowed and, if so, who may

administer it. There is a strong movement in many states to disallow corporal punishment in favor of other alternatives for student discipline. Teachers can be held legally liable for assault and battery in civil courts for excessive physical punishment that may injure a child.

Suspension and Expulsion. Because states require compulsory school attendance and provide free education, the courts recognize the right to an education as a student's "property right under the Fourteenth Amendment." Suspending students from school arbitrarily deprives the student of this right. To be able to remove such a right, the teacher or staff member must give the student due process before he or she administers any disciplinary action. When a teacher administers disciplinary actions against a student with special needs, the action must be judged in light of the student's disability and overall behavior pattern.

Generally, only school boards can expel a student from school. The U.S. Supreme Court addressed the due process rights of students in suspensions in *Goss v. Lopez,* 1975. Students facing temporary suspensions of less than 10 days must be given notice of why they are being suspended and the opportunity to tell their side of the story. The Court also stated that, if a student is threatened with a suspension longer than 10 days, more elaborate procedural safeguards might be necessary. It is advisable for the substitute to ask the school principal or assistant principal for a copy of the student code of conduct and disciplinary policies and procedures.

Search and Seizure. The Court has recently handed down decisions related to the schools and the Fourth Amendment dealing with student searches for drugs and weapons. The Supreme Court in *New Jersey v. T.L.O.,* 1985, has detailed the requirements for school searches of students or their lockers, backpacks, and cars. School law attorneys do not recommend that teachers conduct student searches. They must contact the school principal if such need arises.

Religion. The First Amendment of the U.S. Constitution mandates, in part, the Congress not make laws establishing religion or prohibiting religious practices. Based on this amendment, subsequent court cases

145

direct schools to maintain a neutral position toward religion in all their dealings. A student may not interfere with the religious practice of other students. Current legal issues involving religion include distribution of religious literature on school campuses, released and shared time for religious instruction, religious holidays, use of school facilities for religious purposes during noninstructional hours, the use of "moments of silence" for meditation to replace prayers at school, and the use of prayer at school-sponsored functions.

Child Abuse. A person who has reasonable cause to know or suspect that a child has been subjected to abuse or neglect, or who has observed a child being subjected to circumstances or conditions that would reasonably result in abuse or neglect, including self-abuse, must immediately report this information to the school employee (teacher, counselor, school nurse, principal, or social worker) who will in turn acquire firsthand knowledge of the facts, then report such information to the county's or state's child protective services or the appropriate state authority.

Some states require teachers to report suspected child abuse directly to a state agency. Most states provide immunity from law suits for teachers who report suspected child abuse as long as the teacher does not knowingly and maliciously give false information. The substitute should ask the school principal for the specific teacher-reporting procedures in that school.

Sexual Harassment. All educators are expected to conduct themselves in such a way that no staff member or student may feel pressured by sexual advances, requests for sexual favors, or other verbal or physical conduct of a sexual nature that could be construed to be sexual harassment. In most schools, administrators discourage teachers from touching students for any purpose, even a reassuring pat on the back. It is advisable that teachers do not sit children in their laps, be alone in the classroom with a student, or transport a student alone in the teacher's car.

Liability

Though it is never desirable to dwell on unpleasant occurrences, due to the amount of litigation occurring in education today, it may be wise, as most teachers do, to purchase liability insurance. This insurance protects you from costs of litigation over an incident that occurs in school. Many professional educational organizations sell employment liability policies to their members or include the policy as part of their annual dues. In addition, some homeowner's insurance policies may be expanded to provide such coverage. A number of items may be included: awards for damages arising out of teacher activities; attorney fees; bail bond; and assault-related personal property damage. Find out what your liabilities are and how the school district handles coverage for teachers. Then seek coverage for yourself so that you will be comfortable in knowing that you have prepared in the best way you know how to protect your personal and financial assets.

Your Plan of Action

Substitutes are in a position to see the best of what is happening in schools. You can adapt and adopt the very best from all that you observe as you move from one teacher's room to the next. This can be a liberating and enlightening experience. Take advantage of it.

Use this book as the basis for your exploration into the life of your local schools. Add to the information here to make you a better teacher. You may wish to read further from the authors listed in the bibliography, a good source for many references on specific topics.

You are in the classroom to provide professional help to the regular teacher when he or she is absent, and to be able to carry on the learning that follows the teacher's plans rather than simply to respond to crises or drift until the end of the class period or day. You are there to excite students to learn, develop self-esteem, acquire self-control, and be the best possible persons they can be. You are in charge.

To be as challenging a substitute teacher as possible, you must examine professional alternatives and thoughtfully choose the best course of action most likely to handle the situation and achieve the teacher's goals. You have already made a good start!

Glossary

Activity center A defined area in the elementary or middle school classroom for students to play and develop. Examples include a housekeeping or homemaking center, a block center, a dramatic play center, a sand/water table, and a manipulatives center.

Authentic assessment Evaluation of students' progress with consideration toward development of real-life, meaningful, useful skills. Types include open-ended questions, performance tasks, anecdotal recordkeeping, use of checklists, narrative report cards, journals, portfolios, conference, audio and/or video taping. The process the student completes is as important as the end-product.

Collaboration Act of cooperation in which two or more teachers plan together to deliver a curriculum that meets the individual needs of students, such as a special education teacher planning with a general education teacher to prepare activities to meet the needs of special education students in that classroom.

Cooperative learning Heterogeneous grouping of students for classroom activities—social and/or academic—wherein students in the group work together, or cooperate, to complete the assignment. Size of group, group member roles, appropriateness of the assignment for a group, and time allocation are all important factors to consider when using cooperative education.

Core competencies Basic skills of a particular content area that a student must acquire to function adequately in society. Includes reading, writing, listening, communicating, and computational, problem-solving, analyzing, critical thinking, and human relations skills.

Core subjects Include the four content areas in the curriculum that make up a major portion of a student's studies: English, math, science, and social studies. Sometimes these are coherently integrated with a similar theme or common thread.

Departmentalizing A format in which teachers (frequently in grades 4, 5, and 6) have a homeroom class to which they teach a given subject (such as reading), and then they teach one other subject (science, social studies, math, or English) in which they specialize. The rest of the day students either "change classes" or the teachers move from room to room. This method reportedly brings better instruction to students in all content areas and encourages young students to learn responsibility to several teachers and teaching styles.

Developmentally appropriate practices Using activities, materials, strategies, and techniques with students that are suitable for their age and/or developmental level. Attention to individual needs and development is very important in helping each child learn. A child development psychology text or an early childhood education text will provide more theories and ideas related to child development.

Facilitator/guide Teachers are no longer authoritarian directors of classrooms in many areas. Instead, they plan appropriate activities, introduce them, and then take on the role of facilitator or guide in assisting students as they need help completing assigned tasks. Teachers answer questions, help students help themselves, observe students at work, and generally monitor the classroom.

Grouping strategies Teachers group students in a variety of ways, depending on the activity involved and the age and/or developmental level of students. Some examples include pairing or learning buddies, small group, and large or whole group for reading, problem solving, discussion, or projects.

Inclusion Settings in which special education students are placed in a regular classroom for most or all of the time on a continuing basis. Special education teachers then collaborate or plan with the regular classroom teacher and may team teach with the regular teacher to meet the needs of the special education students in that classroom.

Instructional delivery models Different methods of teaching students, including lecture, cooperative learning, individual research project, debate or discussion, inquiry, concept attainment, synectics, and case studies.

Interdisciplinary Frequently applicable at the middle school and secondary levels, but also at times at the elementary level, in which teachers combine materials from two or more academic or curriculum areas for a period of time to provide a blended study, such as studying an integration of American history and American literature from the same time periods.

Integrated Synonymous with interdisciplinary. Integrated is a term used more for this method when used in the elementary grades and applies to the blending of content from two or more areas of the curriculum to provide a more real-life, meaningful study.

Learning centers A defined area of the classroom developed with materials from one or more curriculum areas as a base (frequently integrated now). Rather than being used for remedial work or enrichment when students finish their work, today learning centers provide support for and development of understanding regarding one or more of the particular content areas currently under study. These centers, unlike activity centers, change as the unit of study changes.

Multiage Multigraded Nongraded Ungraded Represent a method of grouping students in classrooms where two or more ages or grade levels of students are combined with a teacher to provide a more developmentally appropriate atmosphere in which students can comfortably develop at their own natural rates without stigmas or fear of "failing."

Team teaching Arrangement in which two or more teachers teach the same students together during the same time period. This process requires combined planning time, willingness to work with each other, and complementary teaching styles.

Thematic curriculum Broad units of study that center on or around themes, questions, or sets of related topics. Methods of thematic instruction are varied and under current study.

Whole language A philosophy—rather than a method or strategy—of teaching that blends components of literacy and language with other parts of the curriculum, such as combining all parts of one content area such as the language arts (reading, grammar, writing, and spelling), or combining parts of language arts (or as many as possible) with other curriculum areas. Whole language activities involve many hands-on, purposeful, child-centered, fun activities that usually include children's literature, art, writing, listening, reading, thinking, and sharing.

Annotated Bibliography

General Reference-Substitute Teacher

Adler, M. J. 1982. *The Paedeia proposal: An educational manifesto.* New York: Macmillan.

Outlines Adler's proposals for a system of instruction based on the Paedeia schools.

Blachowicz, C. L. Z. 1993. Subframe: A strategies planning frame for substitute teachers. *Journal of Reading* 37(3): 234–35.

A five-step generic frame for a reading lesson plan, which is an excellent model for substitutes to use in planning lessons in any subject.

Davis, D. 1980. Subcenter: Have folders, will travel. *Instructor* 90(2): 36.

Offers a method of organizing portable files of resources, ideas, activities and materials pertaining to specific subject matter and various grade levels, which can be quickly selected when a substitute assignment has been accepted.

Freedman, M. K. 1975. The new substitutes: Free to teach. *NASSP Bulletin* 59(391): 95–98.

A New York city study indicated that substitute teachers were less effective than teacher aides or student teachers; therefore, eight suggestions were offered, including having the substitute prepare one exceptional lesson that could be given to every class if the teacher had not left easily followed lesson plans.

Gardner, H. 1983. *Frames of mind: The theory of multiple intelligences.* New York: Basic Books.

Based on Gardner's work in exploring different types of intelligence and means to develop multiple intelligences in students.

Hicks, D. E. 1987. Whose sub is she anyway? *Instructor* 97(3): 79–80.

Helpful tips that allow the substitute and students both to have a productive and pleasant day are provided. It discusses a supportive school staff that gives the substitute greater confidence.

Johnson, J. M., M. Holcombe, and K. Vance. 1988. Apprehensions of substitute teachers. *The Clearing House* 62(2): 89–91.

A research study of the apprehension of substitute teachers regarding their roles. Many substitute teachers did not seem to be very anxious generally; however, they did worry about a variety of factors related to substituting.

Platt, J. M. 1987. Substitute teachers can do more than just keep the lid on. *Teaching Exceptional Children* 19(2): 28–31.

Materials and procedures developed to help substitute teachers who work with learning disabled resource rooms are described. Though many schools no longer have such facilities, the information could be helpful for working with learning disabled students. It discusses specific student information, classroom procedures, daily plans, and alternative activities.

St. Michel, T. 1994. Substitute teachers: Who? what? how? when? where? why? A case study of the substitute process. Unpublished doctoral dissertation, Tempe, Arizona State University.

St. Michel, T. 1995. *Effective substitute teaching: Myth, mayhem, or magic?* Thousand Oaks, Calif.: Corwin Press.

A three-pronged study in which teachers, students, and substitutes were interviewed and observed to review the process for acquiring, training, and keeping substitutes, in order to prepare a training model for district substitute teachers.

Trotter, A., and T. Wragg. 1990. A study of supply teachers. *Research Papers in Education* 5(3): 251–76.

A British journal article that discusses a taped interview of 20 supply teachers—the English name for substitute teacher—asking them to react to the job of supply teacher, how they handled the first meeting of class, and how they responded to disruptions in the classroom. More disadvantages than advantages were presented.

Westling, D. L., and M. A. Koorland. 1988. *The special educator's handbook.* Boston: Allyn and Bacon.

A comprehensive overview of the life of a special education teacher with more than 100 suggestions highlighted for easy reference. Particularly helpful are the chapters on individual and group planning, selecting and using instructional material, using behavior management techniques and other techniques, and working with administrators and supervisors.

Discipline

Albert, L. 1989. *A teacher's guide to cooperative discipline: How to manage your classroom and promote self-esteem.* Circle Pines, Minn.: American Guidance Service.

An easy-to-use K–12 plan that integrates an understanding of a student's behavior with practical discipline techniques. Numerous interventions and strategies are selected based on observations developed from a "School Action Plan."

Burke, K. 1992. *What to do with the kid who . . . Developing cooperation, self-discipline, and responsibility in the classroom.* Palatine, Ill.: IRI/Skylight Publishing.

Blending research and personal experience, teachers and staff developers prepared 200 problem-solving strategies for all grade levels. These strategies are divided into four areas: lack of responsibility, weak interpersonal skills, serious behavior problems, and special needs students.

Canter, L., and M. Canter. 1976. *Assertive discipline: A take-charge approach for today's educator.* Los Angeles: Canter & Associates.

Teachers can assertively take charge of their classes using Canter's five steps, including teachers positively explaining their expectations using consistent rewards and consequences.

Charles, C. M., and G. W. Senter. 1992. *Building classroom discipline,* 4th ed. White Plains, N.Y.: Longman.

This resource provides an overview of classroom discipline and misbehavior with a look at specific preventive, supportive, and corrective procedures. Eight differing models for classroom management are concisely described with suggestions for integrating them into personal teacher models that fit their individual personalities, philosophies, and classrooms.

Curwin, R. L., and A. N. Mendler. 1988. *Discipline with dignity.* Alexandria, Va.: Association for Supervision and Curriculum Development.

A realistic, practical approach describing classroom responsibilities, providing insight into school and student problem situations with 12 specific processes that contribute to sound discipline.

Glasser, W. 1992. *The quality school: Managing students without coercion.* New York: Harper.

Post-1985 Glasser approach helps teachers change their ways of working with students, becoming leaders in a noncoercive and nonadversarial environment while meeting students' needs for belonging, power, fun, and freedom.

149

Jones, F. H. 1987. *Positive classroom discipline*. New York: McGraw-Hill.

> A practical, comprehensive look at the interrelatedness between techniques of classroom discipline, instruction, and motivation are analyzed with numerous secondary examples.

Mendler, A. N. 1992. *What do I do when . . . ? How to achieve discipline with dignity in the classroom*. Washington, D.C.: National Educational Service.

> Practical guidance in how to discipline effectively while respecting a student's dignity, along with principles of effective discipline and strategies for handling them.

Reissman, R. 1993. Hot topic: Creative solutions to discipline dilemmas. *Learning* 22(4): 48–50.

> A number of potentially difficult situations are identified—i.e., defiant disruptives, noncombatant noncompliers, and incessant interrupters—and the best way for positively and creatively handling them is described.

Santa-Rita, E. 1993. *Classroom management for student retention*. New York: Bronx Community College.

> A guidebook looking at seven different approaches for providing greater teacher-student interaction as a means of keeping students focused and preventing discipline problems.

Stanley, S. 1991. Substitute teachers can manage their classrooms effectively. *NASSP Bulletin* 75(532): 84–88.

> A guideline for substitute teachers that identifies four research-supported points, including: arrive early to obtain necessary administrative information; maintain firm control of the classroom; clarify student behavior expectations; and help students understand the importance of learning.

Swick, K. J. 1991. *Discipline: Toward positive student behavior—What research says to the teacher*. Washington, D.C.: NEA Professional Library.

> An overview of discipline with a suggestion for making students more sensitive to the intricacies of the world in which they learn and develop. The last section of the book looks at proposed strategies for responding to discipline in the school.

Wilson, K. G. 1985. Guidelines for substitute teachers in secondary schools. *NASSP Bulletin* 69(479): 73–76.

> Guidelines for a good teaching environment include: a good lesson plan, expect the unexpected, use staff and students as a resource, improvise relevantly, use technology, and enforce discipline promptly.

Wong, H. K., and R. T. Wong. 1991. *The first days of school*. Sunnyvale, Calif.: H. K. Wong Publications.

> Discipline in the classroom is based on three principles: expect your students to be successful, develop good classroom management skills, and design effective lessons so students will succeed. The book has many specific suggestions to accomplish these three goals.

Elementary Education

Donahue, P. 1986. Secrets of a substitute. *Early Years* 17(August/September): 66–67.

> Effective classroom management helps provide a good substituting experience for both students and teacher. To help with this, a number of topics are discussed including lesson plans, examples of student materials and activities, seating charts, and class rules and procedures.

Gray, D. 1981. Seventeen tips to put added zip in your teaching. *Early Years* 10(November): 59–62.

> Though an old journal issue, the tips are still timely for the substitute.

Pronin, B. 1983. Guerilla guide to effective substitute teaching. *Instructor* 92(6): 64–66.

> Substitute teachers who know what to expect and how to handle difficulties perform a great educational service. Suggestions on how substitutes can introduce themselves, gain the respect of the class, and avoid discipline pitfalls are given. "Sub Surprises"—classroom games and other interesting activities that help motivate students—are listed.

Secondary Education

Benedict, K. C. 1987. Student expectations and the substitute teacher. *The Clearing House* 61(1): 27–28.

> It is suggested that the substitute give the students a questionnaire to determine their expectations for the class, thus inviting them to be in control of their learning, lowering barriers that prevent learning. Tips for writing a questionnaire are provided.

Maitland, L. 1984. When the teacher's away, the students will learn. *American Biology Teacher* 46(5): 275–78.

> Guidelines for preparing a lesson based on a topic of general interest using an audio-cassette and worksheet are presented. The example used is coping with death.

Meyer, P. 1984. The social studies substitute. *Social Studies Review* 23(3): 38–40.

> Successful impromptu lessons and activities used in secondary social studies classes are shared by this substitute. Some of them address skills needed by all social studies students.